What ev
needs to know

"In an easy-to-read, jargon-free book Cathy Tsang-Feign helps confront problems unique to the expatriate experience."

-South China Morning Post

On the principle that "awareness is half the cure," psychologist Cathy Tsang-Feign identifies and explains most of the common personal, relationship and family problems encountered by people living abroad: from the initial culture shock to the special joys and pitfalls of the expatriate experience, to the challenges of re-entering your own native country.

In this thoroughly-revised and expanded new edition, Dr. Tsang-Feign uses real-life examples and easy-to-understand explanations to fully prepare you for a move abroad, and to help those already there to help themselves live a well-rounded, satisfying life.

Disclaimer

First published as Self-Help for Foreigners, 1993
Republished as Keeping Your Life, Family and
  Career Intact While Living Abroad, 1996
Third Revised Edition, 2013

ISBN 978 962 7866 18 3

pomelo publishing
pomelopub.com
a division of stvdio media

Cover illustration by Alfredo Martinez
alfredomartinezillustration.com

Other illustrations by Larry Feign

For updates:
livingabroadbook.com

Keep Your Life, Family and Career Intact While
LIVING ABROAD

Third edition, revised and expanded

Cathy Tsang-Feign, PhD

To love and to treasure -

dedicated to my husband Larry,

who untiringly helped make this book come true.

Contents

Acknowledgements

I first thank my clients, who are the source of my inspiration. Each has gone through pain and struggle in striving to become a happy and healthy individual. It is my privilege to work with them. I have learned from each and every one because they were willing to trust me.

My special thanks and gratitude go to my husband Larry for his patience, support and assistance in editing and putting the manuscript together. Without his love, encouragement and all-around helpfulness this book would never have been a reality.

Foreword

THERE IS A lot of romance associated with living abroad. It is often seen as a life of glamour, of white suits and high tea on palm-shaded verandas, chauffeurs and servants and dinners with diplomats, with no problems in store other than a touch of culture shock.

This naïve fantasy might be expected of one who has read too many popular novels about Paris or Shanghai. But all too often, it is held by those actually living abroad as expatriates. When this fanciful image is finally shattered by the realities of life in a foreign land, the disappointment can be overwhelming.

Living in another culture can be extremely rewarding, both financially and personally. It is a special lifestyle. As such, it comes with special problems: stress, acculturation, isolation, long-distance relationships, bored or frustrated wives, oft-traveling husbands, and rootless children.

Frequently these problems are predictable, if not inevitable. Often they take us by surprise. For many people, these special "expat" problems can lead to a general feeling of confusion and alienation in the foreign society. In the worst cases, they can lead to the break-up of marriages that had always seemed happy before moving abroad.

This book is intended to help all those who live, for whatever reasons, in a foreign country. It is intended for expatriates, immigrants, and those planning such a move.

1

On the principle that "awareness of the problem is half the cure," this book identifies and explains, by way of example, most of the common personal, relationship and family problems encountered by people living far away from home. From the initial culture shock, to the special joys and pitfalls of life as a foreigner, to the particular problems suffered by men, women and children overseas, to the unforeseen traumas of re-entering your own native country.

Using real-life examples and easy-to-understand, jargon-free explanations, this book aims to more fully prepare people for a move abroad, and to help those already there to help themselves live a well-rounded, satisfying life.

Awareness is half the cure

Many clients walk into my office and tell me: "I'm miserable. I know something isn't right in my life. How can I fix it?"

"Fixing" something is only a matter of time, approach or method. The real issue for most people is not that they have a problem that needs fixing, but that they end up repeating the same mistakes over and over again.

The main purpose of this book is to help you detect your problem areas, look for patterns and confront them. Before you can ask a question like, "What should I do now?", you need to ask yourself what you are doing, and how your own actions or thinking have contributed to or help to maintain self-destructive patterns. Until then nothing can alter the problem.

Sometimes people try to run away from reality by changing place, job or partner. They hope a "fresh start" will make the problem go away. But the fact is: no matter how many times you relocate, change jobs or remarry, you ultimately cannot run away from yourself.

Whether or not you stay in one specific place or with one partner, you still need to live with yourself. But you do have a choice: you can either continue to be dissatisfied, or you can choose to approach life in a different way. Many people go for years without being conscious of how much they themselves are to blame in creating their own problems, or how they have allowed other people to manipulate them.

Awareness is half the cure—When you are aware of your own actions, you will understand what purpose your undesirable behavior is serving. Once you gain this understanding, you are less likely to slip into old patterns. If you do end up repeating old habits, you will be more aware of what you do and can make a conscious effort to tackle them.

There are no "cures" or magic in this book. What I have done is to define and explain common complaints of people who live overseas, to help you discover, prevent and avoid similar pitfalls in your own life. Human beings are very flexible. If you want to, you will and you can alter your life by yourself, armed with an understanding of the root causes of your habits, patterns and problems. That is the goal of this book—to reach people who are sincere and serious in wanting to do something for themselves.

As individuals we all have the right to live a full and satisfying life. It is up to you to exercise that choice.

Chapter 1

Problems of moving

MOVING EXPERIENCES

MOVING OVERSEAS OFFERS one of the most exciting opportunities any person can ever experience. Whether one is moving abroad by choice or by assignment, there is much to look forward to: travel, exotic cultures, foods and languages. And, naturally, things to worry about: health, climate, homesickness, and the unfamiliar and unknown.

If one has never lived in a foreign country before, it is hard to imagine what it will be like. But even for those who have relocated two or three times, each move is different, promising new pleasures and new pains.

Moving to another country is a stressful experience, whether the move is permanent or for a specific period of time. Most people move for positive reasons, such as career transfer, starting a better life abroad, or sheer wanderlust. They look forward to the change of scenery with anticipation and excitement. Yet as the departure date looms nearer, tiny doubts and anxieties begin to add up to mental and physical stress. Such concerns are normal, even predictable. They are best dealt with before the move rather than after.

STRESS BEFORE THE MOVE

Lilian, age 34, will be moving to Australia with her husband and daughter in six months. For over three weeks she has been suffering from insomnia. She saw her physician, who referred her for psychotherapy.

Lilian says she used to be an easy-going person. But during the past several weeks she found herself moody and frequently snapping at her husband. She has lost interest in and is unable to concentrate on her job.

"I don't know why I should feel so anxious. I thought I was all prepared for the move," she said.

Lilian's reaction is not surprising. She is going through a major change in life and is unable to cope with the stress involved. Not understanding what she is going through makes her even more anxious and unable to deal with it in an appropriate manner.

Moving abroad is a stressful event which demands a great deal of emotional strength. Many factors contribute to such stress.

First, one has to deal with a major restructuring of the family. Separation from relatives can stir up enormous sadness and guilt, especially when elderly parents are being left behind. This may be taken as disloyalty or abandonment, which can be particularly stressful for people from certain cultural or religious backgrounds, such as Asians or Catholics, because of their traditional emphasis on family and the elderly. For the ones leaving this is a double blow. They have to adjust to the loss as well as bear the guilt.

Guilt doesn't resolve problems but merely compounds them. Directly expressing one's feelings to family members will help clarify misunderstandings and open channels for mutual support. All have to give each other time to accept and adapt to the change, and must realize that separation is a growth process which has benefits as well as drawbacks.

Another major stress factor for people about to move is fear of the future in a foreign land. Neither Lilian nor her husband has ever been to Australia. Yet they have already said their goodbyes and rented out their home. There is no question of turning back. But still their unfamiliarity with Australia is creating uncertainty and anxiety.

Frequent bombardment of advice from family and friends can also be quite exhausting and stressful. Though offered with good intentions, most advice tends to focus on the negative. Departees will be told over and over how to prepare for the strange climate, the unavailability of safe, familiar food, and so on. Such warnings only increase apprehension and doubt. Since advice is often conflicting, it can further confuse and overwhelm the already nervous traveler.

People preparing to move overseas have to take advice with a grain of salt. Use your own judgment and wisdom when listening to suggestions. If necessary, gently tell your enthusiastic advisors to step back and give you time to work through it.

The stress of the process of moving abroad cannot be eliminated. However, if appropriate steps are taken it can be minimized.

Usually there are thousands of chores requiring attention prior to the actual move. It is easy to become overwhelmed and confused. Thus it is helpful to prioritize tasks, make lists, and tackle chores one at a time. This not only helps to actually get everything done, but will increase your feeling that things are under control. In order to reduce the anxiety of moving to a new place it is advisable to make a visit prior to the actual relocation.

It is important for you to be aware of your own mechanisms of responding to stress. Instead of repressing the anxious feelings it helps to verbalize them with your spouse, family members or friends. Through communication, you will find mutual support to deal with the coming separation and uncertainty.

You should not worry if you feel "not totally prepared". Everyone feels this way. As long as you understand what you are going through and don't let the anxiety and stress take over, you will be able to effectively complete the chores and preparations, and better deal with the emotional changes.

Individuals in Lilian's situation need to realize that the stress and confusion they experience are normal. They are part of an adjustment process that will eventually come to an end. You have to accept and deal with it rather than reproach yourself for feeling that way. Given time and an open mind you will have few problems in making the transition to the new land.

CULTURE SHOCK

After selling or letting the house, shipping the furniture, and attending the farewell parties, most people feel they are all ready to go. However, moving abroad requires more than just physical preparations.

An individual or family relocating overseas is about to undergo tremendous changes in their life. Besides the normal adjustments associated with moving—setting up house, finding new friends, familiarizing themselves with new geography and climate—new expatriates face a host of other changes.

They will be intrigued—and repelled—by new sights, sounds, smells, and ways of thinking and living. Changes in cultural identity, social position and etiquette will all take getting used to. Foreign languages, dress, food and customs are all part of the excitement and challenge of moving to a new land.

An individual cannot help but react to all the new stimuli and influences in his or her life. The reaction is not a single event, but a mixture and series of emotions, ranging from elation to depression to infatuation to homesickness. This mixed bag of reactions is commonly known as "Culture Shock".

Most people who move overseas expect to experience this phenomenon. Many believe it is something like jetlag: an adjustment you go through and get over with within a short period of time. In fact, the experience is better defined as *acculturation,* a process which can last from six months to more than a year.

Anyone who moves to another country will inevitably go through acculturation. Immigrants expect to take on a new cultural identity and therefore are more willing to adjust and adapt. However, expatriates planning to stay only a set period of time usually have no intention to assimilate. For them, acculturation can be as unpleasant as it is unexpected.

"I've only been here four months, yet I just can't wait until my home leave in December!"

Benjamin, a marketing buyer, was transferred to Hong Kong on a two-year contract. A few weeks ago he began to complain about the crowds, the weather, not being understood by his staff, and so on. All he talks about is how much better things were back home. He is homesick.

What Benjamin is going through is the normal process of acculturation. But like him, many people are taken by surprise when it happens.

Whether people choose to or not, they will go through four stages of acculturation. These are:

ELATION: When first in a foreign country, one finds it quite stimulating that most things are so unlike back home. For Benjamin, the exotic Asian sights and sounds and meeting the lively international expatriate crowd were all part of the initial excitement. However, after several weeks, when one has to settle down to everyday life, the differences can turn into annoyances.

RESISTANCE: Frequent comparisons between home and the host country make everything back home seem so much better.

Benjamin is getting annoyed by the frantic pace of life in Hong Kong, the indirectness of Chinese people in business, the crowds and difficulties in being understood. He is frustrated at the narrow choice of English-language entertainment on television or in cinemas and theaters. He finds himself missing his old friends, favorite foods, and the ways of doing things back home.

11

Many foreigners in this stage tend to associate only with others from their own country. They constantly compare everything to "back in England" (or New York or Frankfurt). Such people remain separate from the local community and establish their own secluded, privileged society. Many expatriates remain in this stage until the day they move back home.

TRANSFORMATION: Usually this occurs about nine months down the road, when individuals feel more familiar with the environment and begin to see the good side of the host country.

For example, Benjamin will probably appreciate the efficiency of service and be intrigued by many Asian customs and formalities, which he finds so much more attractive and sophisticated than back home.

Often, people in this stage go to the extreme of rejecting their own culture. Immigrants in particular may try to take on a totally new cultural identity. They refuse to speak their native language or associate with their own countrymen. They tend to view their own culture with a negative attitude and disdain its customs and traditions as backward or crude.

As for expatriates, after months of adjustment they now appreciate the privileged and exciting expat lifestyle: travel, cultural variety, domestic help, etc. They embrace life overseas, no longer wanting to return to the "average", "boring" lifestyle back home. They may put down people back home whom they see as naïve or narrow-minded. Many get stuck in this stage. They either stay put in this particular expatriate society or move to another foreign country so as to maintain their expatriate lifestyle.

However, no matter how much a person changes outwardly, he cannot shed his roots. Culture is embedded in a person's thinking and behavior. One simply cannot shed one's cultural roots and transform into a different person.

Ideally, people continue the natural course of acculturation to the final stage.

INTEGRATION: Cultural barriers are bridged. Individuals finally learn to appreciate both their own heritage and the new way of life.

Many people remain stuck in the second or third stages, Resistance or Transformation, cutting themselves off from either their new world or the one they came from. These "adjustments" are unbalanced, and lead to eventual frustration and unhappiness. Many of the difficulties and psychological complaints of foreigners in a new land, including stress and family problems, can be directly linked to incomplete acculturation.

Children usually are more easily acculturated or assimilated than adults. The different paces of adjustment to the new culture can put a gap between parent and child. Therefore, parents should not overlook this area.

If expatriates and new immigrants understand and anticipate the four stages of acculturation, much of the stress and turmoil of relocation can be dealt with. Particularly during the second stage, newcomers like Benjamin need to give themselves time for adjustment and not give up and go home.

TRANSIENT FAMILY SYNDROME

For immigrants and most expatriates, acculturation is a temporary but necessary process, enabling them to feel at home in a new land. But for a third group of people, it is a never-ending routine, leaving them feeling that they have no home at all.

Growing numbers of families—diplomatic, missionary, military and, increasingly, business people—are required to move on a regular basis, usually every two or three years, to a new, distant location. Such families are often the envy of relatives and friends. Yet underneath the glamour and excitement of the globetrotting lifestyle lies a host of pitfalls and problems. These people are often reluctant to voice their complaints, for fear that others wouldn't understand, or of jeopardizing their own or their spouse's career.

Ever since Lucy returned from visiting her sister's family in the United States, she finds herself moody and unhappy. Whenever her husband tries to comfort her she lashes out at him.

"I enjoy our lifestyle and I wouldn't trade it for anything, but I also never knew how much I was missing," Lucy said.

Lucy moved to Taiwan six months ago. Prior to that, she lived in Egypt, Poland and Greece. Because of her husband's diplomatic career. they are required to relocate frequently. Taipei is their fourth posting in the past ten years.

"I never could imagine how my sister lived her mundane suburban life. Now I understand there are many rich experiences that I cannot have," she said.

Seeing her sister's stable home life, house, close friends and friendly neighbors, she has suddenly realized how much these things mean to her.

Lucy enjoys her varied life, living in different parts of the world, yet all of a sudden she feels that she wants something more than "interesting experiences". After all these years Lucy finds herself with no close friends, no place that feels like home. As much as they call the United States "home", she doesn't really feel their roots are there anymore.

Lucy's dilemma is a result of "Transient Family Syndrome". People like her are planning their next move almost as soon as they arrive at their latest assignment. Although they will establish an active social life, when any relationship becomes too personal or emotionally involved, unintentionally they pull back. Rather than going through the repeated pain of separation and loss, they unconsciously avoid letting friendships get too close.

In addition, people in this group tend to associate with others who, like them, also transfer frequently. Living among such a transient population is not conducive to forming close, lasting relationships.

Transient Family Syndrome is especially hard on spouses. Since one person's career requires frequent moves, the partner cannot fully develop her or his own career or outside interests. In Lucy's case, she doesn't have the chance to be a normal homemaker. She doesn't have the time needed to build bonds or support with neighbors. She is unable to take root in the local community and establish a close circle of friends. When she is feeling down she doesn't have someone to call upon or a shoulder to cry on. "At times I feel terribly lonely," Lucy claims. She has no outlets outside of her husband and children.

This problem not only affects individuals, but the whole family. With no outside support, family members put tremendous demands on each other and expect the marriage and family life to meet all emotional needs. Such families often become so interdependent that individual outside friendships may seem like "treason". This feeling inhibits them even more from other contacts, which results in further isolation. The effective way to deal with Transient Family Syndrome is not relocating back home, but finding the courage to open up emotionally and reach out to establish genuine friendships.

It is true that distance can create obstacles to sustaining close friendships. However, if mutual effort is made to stay in touch, such obstacles can be conquered. Phone or video calls, e-mails, posting little gifts, and occasional visits can keep friendships alive. Your attitude can overcome the problem of distance.

Members of transient families need to be aware of whether they are in any way sabotaging each other's personal growth. It is important for them to give space to each other and encourage outside contacts. These new friendships will also speed up acculturation.

When such families decide to reach out they will likely find others experiencing similar needs. Nothing will better erase the myth that "we are all alone."

Transient Family Syndrome is not necessarily experienced by all transient families. Yet often an individual or family may not recognize its impact until suddenly it strikes them what they're missing. It is important for people to acknowledge their own feelings and note whether other family members' needs are not fulfilled because of frequent relocations.

EVERY MOVE IS DIFFERENT

No one is immune from the adjustment and stress that come with moving abroad, whether for the first or the fifteenth time. Having experienced relocation once does not make the next move trouble-free. The logistics of moving to a second, third, or fourth overseas assignment will take on a patina of of routine, but it may come as a shock to undergo the inevitable stages of acculturation yet again, to once more find oneself a newcomer, to re-orient oneself to the quirks and subtleties of social and business interactions within a new culture, even if it is just the country next door.

Every move is different, depending on one's life stage or circumstance. Crossing borders after marriage or divorce, or after having children, carries many different contexts, responsibilities and obstacles than a prior relocation when one was young and single or married but childless. A move due to promotion, or starting a new job after a period of unemployment, may distract attention from other personal, social and cultural adjustments.

The problems of moving will at least be familiar the second time around, but it is crucial not to take for granted that less effort is needed to properly settle in. It is important that serial expatriates remind themselves that culture shock, or acculturation, can take from six to nine months, or for some, as long as a year and a half. There are no shortcuts. As long as you are prepared and allow time for the adjustment stages, you are bound to be able to manage well and enjoy a successful assignment abroad.

The international person

Moving to another country, whether for the first or the tenth time, is never an easy experience.

Like a tree transplanted to a new patch of ground, there will be a period of wilting. But given time and a little special care, the transplanted person, like the tree, will recover, acquire greater breadth, and blossom more than ever before.

Coming to terms with one's old and new cultures is coming to terms with two sides of yourself. With sensitivity and an open mind, an immigrant or expatriate can integrate the two and dare to be who he or she really is: a special individual who is truly cross-cultured.

Chapter 2

The expatriate marriage

Marriage abroad

Moving overseas is a family experience. Most people bring their spouse or family with them. Many single expatriates marry in the foreign country, whether to locals or other foreigners. Either way, married life abroad has its own special advantages, as well as its own special problems.

Many couples experience changes in their marriage after moving abroad. Whether the changes are caused by the environment, lifestyle, new economic or social status, or a combination of these, the move can put strain in a relationship. The marriage, just like the individuals in it, has to adapt to the new place.

Both marriage partners must be strong and flexible to deal with the new stresses and strains of a move abroad. A relationship that weathers such changes is a truly loving relationship and will be all the stronger for it.

Foreign affairs

One of the most well-known maxims in any expatriate community is that "Hong Kong (or Rome, or Rio de Janeiro, or (fill in the blank) is a marriage graveyard." It is certainly true that expatriates suffer from a high number of extra-marital affairs and formerly stable marriages suddenly ending in divorce. It is easy, and tempting, to place the blame outward: on the "exotic local girls" or the boredom of being an expatriate wife. But usually the real reasons are to be found by looking inward.

Margaret found out that her husband has been having an affair. "I can't believe he did this to me after I gave up my job, and all my friends, to move overseas for the sake of his career," she said, fighting back tears.

Margaret is 40 years old, married 15 years, with a daughter of 12. Lately she has been suffering from insomnia and depression. "I know our marriage wasn't the best, but it wasn't as bad as he says. Of course, he blames it all on me," she said with a helpless look.

Devastated and confused, Margaret is considering divorce.

Like most people in her situation, Margaret blames the affair for destroying her 15-year marriage. She believes that the novelty and exoticness of the local girls made her husband turn away from his own family. No doubt the affair has contributed to their breaking up, yet it is not likely to be the sole cause. Marital discord doesn't happen overnight. As Margaret recalls: "Bill and I fought a lot over minor things, but I never thought it bothered him that much until he told me recently."

Why did such a thing not occur back home? Why now, after she gave up everything to move abroad with him?

The expatriate lifestyle itself probably served as a catalyst, bringing to the surface, and accelerating, problems that may already have existed in the marriage.

One of the challenges many expatriates face is "identity inflation", in which the image of one's lifestyle leads to unrealistic expectations. Living overseas means being able to enjoy things they never dreamt of having in the past: a glamorous lifestyle, elevated social status, meeting important and interesting people from all over the world, travel, and a live-in maid to take care of domestic chores.

The comfortable lifestyle often leads people to believe everything should be perfect, while deep inside they possess a sense of emptiness. Many wives remark that they don't feel grounded in the new place, that they can never think of the overseas post as "home". They view everything there as temporary. The attachments to "back home" are strong, since most family and friends are still there. The idea of settling down in the foreign land is not appealing at all.

The loss of professional identity compounds the problem. Many women whose spouses are transferred overseas give up their own professional careers to relocate with their husbands. Before, their careers provided a great deal of satisfaction and a sense of achievement. After the relocation, fulfillment is supposed to be through the husband's career and accomplishments. Such a change is not very pleasing.

MARGARET

Margaret gave up her nursing career to move to Hong Kong with her husband, Bill. In doing so, she shifted roles from working mother to full-time home-maker. Now she is facing the possibility of losing even this role because of her husband's affair.

Margaret desperately began looking for things which could give her fulfillment. Her career prospects being limited due to language barriers, she turned to the only outlet available to many expatriate women: volunteer work. She halfheartedly joined some charitable fund-raising activities, hoping it would make her life more meaningful. However, finding a way of passing time doesn't solve the original problem.

Margaret feels as if her identity has been stripped away. Her sense of self-worth is shattered. Even though she enjoys the social status of her husband's position, she sees herself as very much Bill's dependent. She resents this and wishes Bill would give her more support and understanding, after she gave up so much for him.

BILL

Bill, on the other hand, finds his ego boosted daily. He is in his early 40s, but looks younger. He went from being a middle-ranking manager in the home office to a high-ranking executive in the overseas branch, with all the attendant increases in power, status and perks. He enjoys his new powerful identity and all the attention he receives from business associates.

Bill's many business obligations have him working late hours. When he is home, either he is dead tired or he wants to have peace and quiet. Even though Margaret is active socially, she doesn't see her husband all day and is desperate for intimacy. Bill's preoccupation with his job has become the subject of frequent arguments, which makes their relationship even more distant.

Bill is preoccupied with himself and is not able to empathize with Margaret's frustration. He only sees her as unappreciative and views all her complaints as nagging. Meanwhile, Bill unconsciously denies his wife's problem, because resolving it would mean having to alter his glamorous lifestyle.

IDENTITY INFLATION

Again, the expatriate lifestyle creates a type of identity inflation, in which the image distorts reality. But for a career man like Bill, the effect is quite different than for his wife. He has a new, important position in a foreign country. The newness of it gives him a sudden boost of attention and status. He becomes intoxicated on his own feeling of importance, and on the new and exotic.

Returning home at night has become a letdown. There waiting for him are the same old wife, same old children, and same old home routines. Moreover, his wife treats him as the "same old guy", not the special and important "star" his colleagues treat him as.

A man experiencing identity inflation doesn't deliberately set out to have an affair. However, Bill's attention was easily drawn to his local Chinese female subordinate, who is a sympathetic, patient listener and also looks up to him. At the same time, Bill's high-paying job allows him to get all the material comforts he wants. As he puts it, "I work hard and I play hard." These combined factors provide a breeding ground for a fling. In that frame of mind, Bill treats the affair as a reward to himself.

Like most men in this situation, Bill would not admit there is anything wrong with him, let alone seek counseling. Admitting this would be admitting failure, something impossible for a man going through identity inflation to accept. Meanwhile, Bill is having a good time and he doesn't see why he should change the situation, as long as his wife will tolerate it. Terminating the affair is not even considered.

WHO'S TO BLAME?

Margaret blames the affair for destroying her marriage, and the expatriate lifestyle for causing the affair. In fact, she has it backwards.

An affair is usually not the cause of problems within a marriage. More likely, it is a symptom of problems that already exist. The expatriate lifestyle merely aggravates the situation. It is useless to blame the place for problems that arise.

Unfortunately, the burden usually falls on the wife to repair the damage. Margaret needs to tell her husband directly that she knows about the affair, and how she knows. It is advisable that she waits until her first shock is over before discussing it with him. She shouldn't make threats, but clearly state the options and choices they both have.

Husband and wife together must explore the problems in their relationship which may have led to the infidelity. Though the man opened the rift by initiating the affair, marital problems are rarely the fault of one person alone.

After all, marriage is a two-way street. Finally, both need to make a clear and firm choice about where they want their marriage to lead.

A woman in Margaret's situation must work on gaining a better understanding of herself, who she is and what life direction she wants to pursue. Before she can choose between staying married or getting divorced, she needs to regain her sense of self-identity. She needs something to fulfill her intellectually, emotionally and spiritually—something which can give her a sense of self-worth. Finally, she must decide what she wants regarding the future course of her marriage.

Personal growth is vital for every person, of every age group. Indeed, personal growth should be parallel to one's marriage. If one is not happy with oneself, one's marriage is bound to suffer. Every family member needs the opportunity to realize his or her own potential.

WHAT DOES HE REALLY DO ON THOSE BUSINESS TRIPS?

Cases like Bill and Margaret's are the favorite sources of gossip at expatriate social gatherings. No weekend deck party or afternoon tea social would be complete without a fresh story of guess-who's marriage is on the rocks or whispers of so-and-so fooling around with his fashionable young secretary.

One can easily form the impression that marital infidelity is so common among the expatriate community that it is in fact the "norm"; that even the strongest, most stable marriage partnership is under constant siege by myriad temptations.

The ubiquitous gossip can give rise to worries and suspicions that would never have been taken seriously back home. This is especially true when one partner travels frequently. This sort of mistrust can do as much harm to a marriage as an actual adulterous act. In such a climate, assertions of fidelity can even add fuel to the fire of suspicion.

> *"How can I reassure my wife that I don't sleep around during my business trips?" Nathan said. "When I try to explain this, I actually feel guilty, as if saying it makes it sound like I'm trying to hide something."*

Nathan, a business executive, travels frequently on his job. He enjoys his work but feels the job is costing him the trust he once had with his wife. According to Nathan, he and Karen essentially have a good marriage and they have been very trusting and sensitive to each other's needs. However, he senses a barrier slowly growing between them and he is trying to deal with it.

When he returns from his frequent trips, Nathan tries to catch up with his wife and children. At times he feels frustrated at being deprived of a normal family life. Knowing that his wife has to care for the family by herself stirs up guilt in him. He tries to make up for his absences by being more sensitive to her needs and comments. But sometimes her remarks cause him discomfort.

> *"Her girlfriends joke that she should accompany me on my trips. They say she's too trusting. Then she half-kiddingly asks if she should worry."*

Comments like these started off as little jokes, but as Karen repeats them more and more often it is beginning to annoy him. He wonders how serious she is. On a good day he can let it slide, but if he is tired or busy, such remarks provoke unfriendly spats between them.

What Nathan is experiencing is not uncommon among frequent travelers. When a couple spends so much time apart it is reasonable to wonder what the other half is doing. Human beings can be quite imaginative in such situations. The more a partner imagines, the more wild and out of control the thoughts can become. With the spouse not there to clarify all the concerns, it isn't difficult for fleeting fantasy to turn into worried suspicion.

Social pressure can also cause unnecessary alarm. Many spouses are bombarded by stories of other unfaithful partners and what they supposedly do during their business trips. Seeds of doubt are sown in these uncertain home-based spouses. In their minds questions sprout, such as: "I trust my wife but what if...?" or "I trust my husband but I just don't trust the women in some of those places..."

When jokes about suspicion or mistrust get out of hand, this is an alarm signal of potential marital discord. This needs attention right away. As Nathan realizes, it is not easy to open a discussion on "mistrust". If he tries to bring it up to maintain his innocence, she might think he's trying to hide something. But if he says nothing, the suspicions remain. Either way he loses.

Situations like this make even the best marriage vulnerable. And when one spouse is frequently absent, chances to clarify concerns, to work out differences or resolve problems are limited by time. Misunderstanding or unnecessary suspicion on both sides is difficult to avoid. When these feelings accumulate it becomes even harder to share or discuss problems.

The only way to deal with this problem is to confront it. Both husband and wife need to be open and honest in expressing their concerns, annoyances, fears and thoughts. It might be helpful for both partners to quietly write down their thoughts and concerns before talking to one another. By doing so, each can clearly focus on the issue without being sidetracked by the other's reactions and then both can address the problem head-on.

After the issue of mistrust has been discussed, couples need to negotiate ways to reduce these feelings. For example: the traveling partner will allow the spouse to contact them at any time, or the home-based spouse will not pry into personal diaries, and both will limit the "cheating" jokes.

Trust and respect go hand in hand in a marriage. Trust can be built by exercising respect for one another. If trust is based only on promises, it becomes merely an obligation rather than a mutual way of showing love and respect. When people are apart it requires more strength to trust. Trust, like love, is likely to stay alive, provided both are willing to work on it.

FREQUENT FLYER FAMILY FRICTION

Frequent travel can put other strains on a relationship, even when there is no question of suspicion or mistrust. When one partner is away for days or weeks at a time on a regular basis, both have to work harder to maintain intimacy in the marriage.

Obviously, the frequent traveler has many stresses and strains, from the disorientation of moving between time zones to the pressures of accomplishing specific business objectives during a limited time period abroad. Ironically, attempts to provide a happy home for the stressed-out traveler can sometimes do more harm than good to the family.

Elaine cannot help but be affected by her husband's frequent business travel. "I feel I have to tiptoe around Joe before his trips, and again when he comes back."

Both claim they have a happy marriage, in spite of the travel. Yet when he is home, sometimes Elaine finds herself exploding at Joe "over the least little thing." She is confused by her own reactions.

It is obvious that Elaine has bottled up many of her emotions. Prior to his departure she is afraid to bring up anything which may upset him or cause him worry. Her goal is to provide "calm" and "peace" and she makes sure the children don't stir up any trouble either. If anything upsets her she swallows it rather than risk his going away on a sour note.

Upon Joe's return, she requires herself to be cheerful and give a warm welcome regardless of her state of mind. Both expect to have a nice cozy time together after the time apart. Yet this doesn't always happen. Elaine has repressed her feelings to secure peace for Joe's sake. Yet when someone is holding something deep inside, the feelings haven't really gone away. Eventually, like a geyser, they build up and burst out, often triggered by a trivial, and unrelated, event.

For example, in this couple's case, the question of whether Joe will extend his contract for another two years affects both of them. But they both claim they "never seem to have the time" to talk it out fully. There is an intention on both sides to avoid arguments—after all, they don't spend much time together, so why spoil it? Any mention by Elaine on the subject of Joe's contract gets an impatient response of: "Not now." Elaine becomes frustrated and lets it out involuntarily in other ways. In one case, she totally lost her cool when he was twenty minutes late to meet her in town and they stopped speaking all afternoon. Thus, the effort of trying to avoid fights ironically makes arguments and fights inevitable.

When there is tension between them, such couples tend to expect the next business trip will give each a chance to "cool off" and minor disputes to be forgotten. This in turn leads to problems remaining unresolved while they wait for the next separation to provide the "cure".

Frequent travel allows breaks for couples like Joe and Elaine. Yet at the same time it doesn't allow time to share, exchange or even disagree. While apart, they are unable to discuss each other's daily trials and tribulations like most couples would at the end of the day. Yet when Joe returns from a trip, it is almost impossible to backtrack and share a whole list of daily ups and downs with his wife. Instead he chooses to report only a few anecdotes, gossip, and general good news. Ironically, deep inside, a frequent traveler often feels that his spouse either couldn't possibly relate to or doesn't understand the pressures he goes through. Thus he too has many minor pent-up feelings, which sometimes cause him to lash out at Elaine.

Both Joe and Elaine have to recognize that the travel has contributed some uneasiness to the marriage. Joe cannot stop his traveling. But they can start acting more like a normal couple when they're together.

First is to drop the facade that Elaine can't be herself before or after he leaves. Since Joe's travel schedule is unpredictable, couples like this cannot rely on "when he has time" to deal with each other. They need to schedule times together, just like business appointments, both to discuss problems and to just spend quality time with each other. Otherwise all they receive is leftover time.

Secondly, they have to start focusing on specific issues that they have put off discussing, such as Joe's contract. Joe has to share his plans, while Elaine should express her anxiety without exaggerating or acting out. Problems must be dealt with when they arise, not put off until "after the trip".

Lastly is finding time to keep each other updated and openly share thoughts and feelings. After all, Joe works hard to provide for the family, so perhaps the goal to preserve the family needs to be the top task.

The other side of frequent traveling is the home-based spouse who has perhaps adjusted too well to their partner's absences.

"She treats me like an outsider!"

Betsy's husband James is an executive who is on the road two weeks out of every month. Since they relocated abroad nine months earlier, she has been trying to get herself settled. To keep busy during her husband's trips away she built up an active social life for herself and has also become involved in charity fundraising.

Both Betsy and her husband enjoy their time together whenever he is in town. But recently tension has been building up and they often fight over trivial matters. James complains that Betsy is too involved with her friends even when he is in town. He feels she is shortchanging, even ignoring, him. After all, when he is not around she has plenty of time with her friends and volunteer groups. Why should her social life invade their precious and limited time together?

James has a point. It is natural for anybody in his position to expect his wife to give him the highest priority. However, James hasn't realized that lately they live very different lives. Betsy doesn't travel often and has worked hard to build a life for herself. She cannot drop everything whenever he is back in town. She feels he is trivializing her friendships and charity work; in short, trivializing her own needs.

On the other hand, complains Betsy, all James does when he is home is sleep! Much of his time is spent recovering from the exhaustion of travel. Yet he expects her to be there. Sex and intimacy are either nonexistent or scheduled in an unspontaneous way.

What's more, James doesn't hide his disappointment when his homecoming is not greeted with excitement. He is happy and relieved to be home. He can finally unload everything and have a compassionate partner to share with and to listen to him. Yet for Betsy his homecomings are routine matters, His demands for attention are seen as an intrusion into her daily routine. After weeks of running a self-sufficient life, to be a sharing partner also requires time to shift modes.

It is by no means easy for frequent travelers and their families to maintain a "normal" family life. It requires mutual effort to create a workable lifestyle that pleases both partners.

Each partner's feelings should be honored without judging whose feelings are more justified. Such a situation calls for consideration and understanding rather than defending one's position.

James needs to respect Betsy's need to maintain private commitments even when they overlap with his being in town. He can do his part by making his schedule more in line with hers, such as: avoid being away on weekends; plan certain major trips well ahead so that she too has time to set her own schedule and make sure her own free time will coincide with his; once in awhile, arrange for Betsy to join him for a short holiday together when his business abroad is finished.

Betsy of course needs to make more effort to adjust her schedule for her husband's sake. She needs to be sensitive to not treat her spouse like an outsider. Besides adjusting her commitments, when appropriate she should invite him to join with some of her friends and activities, and take no offense if he declines. Finally, let him have some of the enthusiasm he wants from her when he arrives home from an exhausting trip.

In both of the previous examples, it is lack of quality communication that causes problems for a frequent traveler and their spouse. Therefore, communication during the separation is just as essential. It is important to maintain frequent contact by telephone, fax, letters or notes to each other. Inform each other in advance of any special requests, arrangements or other engagements, so that both sides feel prepared.

IMPOTENCE AND POWER STRUGGLES

Communication problems within a marriage are not always so easy to identify or resolve as in the previous cases. Sex is another form of communication within a marriage. Thus, when one partner develops sexual problems, more often than not it indicates other troubles in the relationship.

Many men, for example, find themselves one day suddenly unable to perform sexually with their wives. Ironically, this often occurs around the same time as other more positive changes in their lives, such as a promotion or a transfer overseas. Naturally, the stress of the new job or new environment will be named as the cause. There is usually some truth to this, but not in the way one would expect. As with most marital problems, the cause comes not from without, but from within.

Again, the expatriate lifestyle appears to aggravate, if not give rise to, a problem which may not have existed back home.

Allen is depressed. He claims he has lost all interest in sex and it is affecting his marriage.

Allen, 34, married for over two years, says the first eight months of married life were good. He and his wife were emotionally and sexually compatible. However, two months after they relocated to Tokyo he started experiencing difficulties in having and maintaining erections. He is worried that something is wrong with him. When he finally discussed the problem with his wife, he sensed her frustration as well. She blamed him for "rushing it through and not spending enough time to let it happen." Hearing this only increased his anxiety level.

The depression Allen is experiencing is the natural consequence of his worries about sexual dysfunction. Not knowing how to deal with the problem or understanding what causes it really troubles him. In addition, his wife's reaction confuses him and makes him further doubt himself. It turns into a vicious cycle—the more depressed he is, the worse his problem becomes.

Allen is suffering from secondary impotence. This means at one time he was functioning well, but not at the present moment. Allen is not unusual. In fact, about half of the male population experiences episodes of impotence at one time or another.

Secondary impotence can result from both physical and psychological causes. The former include: stress, fatigue, early undiagnosed diabetes, certain medications and alcohol. The latter include: anxiety, fear of failure and pressure to perform. Marital discord or problems originating in childhood can also aggravate the problem.

Allen's sexual dysfunction must have been triggered by some event in his life. Yet he doesn't seem to know where to trace the factors. "The only difference in our sex life is the frequency," Allen said.

He feels his impotence is inhibiting him from leading a normal sex life with his wife, thus leading to reduced frequency of sex. In fact, it's more likely the other way around. The reduced sex is the cause of his impotence rather than the result.

Since transferring to Tokyo, Allen took up a more prestigious and demanding position in his bank. Usually he is physically and mentally exhausted when he returns home. On the other hand, his wife Wendy, who gave up her career back home to relocate with her husband, has become more dissatisfied and bored. The new-found frustration and jealousy towards her husband's active and busy life creates a sense of insecurity in her.

Without a conscious plan, Wendy tries to maintain her husband's affection and attention through their sexual activities. This is her way of regaining her sense of control and security. However, due to Allen's work responsibilities their time together has been reduced tremendously. The less secure she feels, the more time and greater frequency of sex she demands from Allen.

Her insecurity also affects their sexual activity. She needs more time to achieve orgasm. Her orgasmic problem can likely be attributed to her general frustration. However, from her point of view, her husband is simply impatient with her. This heightens her frustration and complaints.

In the meantime, his fatigue often makes it difficult for him to perform and he ends up losing patience with himself and his wife. Sometimes he views Wendy as demanding something he couldn't give. He finds love-making gradually becoming merely a chore.

Allen tries to maintain a happy married life and keep up with his busy workload as well. Recognizing his wife's needs and frustration, he tries to comfort and be giving. Yet Wendy's orgasmic difficulties inevitably cause him anxiety and fear regarding his sexual performance. His impotence is the result of such pressure.

The first step for Allen is to work on the physical problem—a sex therapist can recommend various exercises which can help treat impotence.

Restoring a strong marital relationship is the most important factor for Allen. Allen's sexual dysfunction is a circular cause and effect, perpetuated by him and his spouse. In order to tackle this problem he needs to involve his wife. It is important for him and his wife to be sensitive to each other to gain an understanding of what triggers the impotence. Hopefully, through such sharing he can also help Wendy to deal with her frustration.

Provided Allen can resolve his psychological pressures, most likely his depression will go away, as will his sexual problems.

Impotence is an ego-threatening problem for most males. It is a treatable problem as long as a man is willing to deal with it directly. With patience, sensitivity, and professional guidance, it can usually be corrected.

Questions and answers
aren't conversations

Trust and respect do not center only around major issues such as sex, marital fidelity or finances. In fact, communication breakdown within a marriage usually originates in more everyday issues.

For example, the way marital partners relate to one another when returning home from work is often a revealing indication of the state of a marriage. One spouse wants to talk, the other doesn't.

This is a very delicate time of the day for any couple, something which most people don't realize. It is particularly sensitive for many expatriate couples. The working expatriate spouse often has greater pressures and longer working hours than back home. Meanwhile, the non-working spouse, usually the wife, is more isolated, often having given up her career, and has fewer contacts with the community than in the past. Thus, when he walks in the door, each needs something very different. Unless handled on both sides with tact, courtesy and respect, those first few minutes home can give rise to hurt and misunderstanding which, if left unresolved, can burn a small but festering wound in an otherwise loving relationship.

"I'm with the kids all day. I don't think I'm asking too much by just wanting some adult conversation," Heidi said.

"How many times do I need to tell you? I don't mean anything personal, but when I walk in the door I'm just not ready to chat," George explained.

As Heidi describes, once George walks in the door she suddenly feels transparent. He goes straight to the living room to read his sports news. For her it is like being doused with cold water.

From George's view, he sees himself walking through the front door into an interrogation room where he is bombarded with questions and mini-crises. He feels overwhelmed and wants to hide.

Who is at fault?

Neither of them. They simply look at things from different angles and don't appreciate each other's point of view. In fact, this is a common phenomenon in many households.

Heidi feels rejected when George returns home, refusing to talk. After all, she spends most of her time with the kids and only at the end of the day can she see George. A little conversation is the least she could expect from him. She questions what she could possibly have done wrong to deserve this kind of treatment. Such feelings inevitably put her in a defensive mode. Sometimes she snaps back to let out her hurt. But usually she will try to win him back by showing keen interest in his work. She will ask all sorts of questions about the office to keep in touch with "his" world.

Once he responds, she will double her enthusiasm and ask more questions.

Yet George takes her questions as another "demand", just like at work. He can't wait until the end of the day so that he can drop his superman/decision maker/negotiator/leader mask. He doesn't want to answer more queries or be at others' disposal. All he wants is to relax and enjoy himself.

Heidi's enthusiasm is taken as an intrusion. He is afraid to open his mouth, for fear of another torrent of words in response. The more chatter his wife makes, the more he keeps her away. He feels Heidi makes conversation only when she is ready to listen and forgets how he feels at that moment.

Furthermore, George thinks he is doing Heidi a favor by not sharing with her. "I don't want to tell her too much about my troubles at work. It will only upset and worry Heidi." He tries to save her from pain by concealing his problems and comes out with bland generalizations.

Whatever George's good intentions, he doesn't realize by doing this he actually makes Heidi more determined to find out what is going on with him. Her constant prying is the result of the worries which he has tried so hard to prevent her from experiencing. What George attempts to avoid eventually comes about from his own doing.

Meanwhile, Heidi has her own needs. Alone all day or with the kids, by evening she is desperate for her husband's companionship, as if his being home is the only fulfilling time in her day. George senses this and feels pressured as a result.

What is happening between Heidi and George is basic misinterpretation of each other's message. When one doesn't know where their partner is coming from it is very easy to misread the situation. This can lead to hurt, anger, and accusations on both sides. It will take some direct clarification and sharing to sort things out.

First, Heidi must understand and respect George's needs. He requires some time to unwind and be himself for a little while before he can be a good companion. Thus, leaving him alone is essential. It will be helpful if Heidi uses that time to do something for herself. A short rest, an evening jog or a phone call to a friend can give her a chance to refresh herself before she shares the evening with her partner.

Likewise, George needs to directly state his thoughts. He should allow his wife to understand him rather than run her around in a game of waiting and guessing. Through direct communication he can save himself and Heidi from trouble and annoyance.

Unless both partners are willing to share their feelings and thoughts, the assumptions they build about each other will become a wall between them. However, sensitivity to each other's feelings will help avoid unnecessary misunderstanding. With a little creative thinking on both sides, the evenings can get off to a good start instead of being unpleasant for everyone.

WIVES WHO LIVE IN FEAR
OF THEIR HUSBANDS

The moment the man walks in the door is not the same for every wife. Most married women, whether they have their own careers or are homemakers, look forward each day to seeing their husbands after work. It may be out of eagerness to share each other's company, or out of relief at having someone else there to help take care of the children and household chores. But for a great many women, the man's homecoming is something to be dreaded. Will he be sweet? Or will he be drunk or in one of his raging moods again?

In most countries, more violence takes place at home than on the street. This is no less true among expatriate communities. The problem of battered expatriate wives is in fact more serious than people are aware of. These women are pressured into silence by the enclosed foreign community, for fear that word may get around which will jeopardize their husband's reputation. Unfamiliarity with local resources keeps them even more isolated. Their situation becomes a vicious trap.

After repeated cancellations, Alice finally showed up for counseling. "He would kill me if he knew I'd talked to you. I don't know what to do anymore. He did promise not to hit me again," Alice sobbed.

Alice, 39, appeared frightened and desperate. She described her husband Jack as "temperamental and anti-social", and physically abusive. Apparently the situation worsened since they moved to Manila nine months ago. He drinks more, and often becomes quite violent. "If I hadn't locked myself in the bathroom the other day he would have killed me," she cried.

Life for Alice is filled with despair. She finds herself walking on thin ice every day. She doesn't know when he will come home in a rotten mood and use her as his punching bag. After most incidents he'll apologize and promise to never let it happen again. Yet sometimes he will be a totally different person and they're able to enjoy some happy moments together.

Alice's situation may seem unbearable to most people. But for her it is still better than having nothing at all. "I need him and I have nowhere to go," she claimed.

Socially isolated and with no family nearby, Alice sees herself as helpless and having no alternative but to depend on Jack. She tolerates his abuse and often finds excuses for his behavior. Either he was "too stressed" or "too drunk" or "still haunted by his deprived family background." Rather than resenting Jack's abuse, she blames herself for causing it. Only after the most recent incident did Alice realize her life was in actual danger. Still, she doesn't recognize his behavior forms a pattern which can only get worse.

People who abuse family members usually are possessive and see their victims as property. They disregard the other person's feelings and are unable to empathize with them. Spouse abuse never happens only once. It is part of a pattern of pathological behavior that is beyond the control of the victim and takes more than a promise to deal with.

A victim of physical abuse often suffers from low self-esteem. She demeans her own self-worth and sees her existence as under the mercy of others. She makes herself feel responsible for the assaulter's behavior. Yet though she may sometimes provoke by being argumentative or nagging, she is not the one actually causing his pathological behavior. Therefore the victim has to first recognize the pattern of such abusive acts and understand that it isn't caused by her own "wrongdoing".

Tolerating abuse will not help the situation, but rather prolong the pain and increase the chances of real danger, not only to the woman but to her children. Usually a drastic move is necessary.

The first thing an abused woman should do is completely remove herself from the situation. She needs a chance to think objectively before any further decisions can be made. It is important for her to re-examine her life and ask herself what she wants out of this relationship. She must decide whether she wants to put up with such abuse or make a new life without her partner.

It isn't easy to gather the courage to break away. Outside help should be sought, but the ultimate decision to change has to come from oneself. Otherwise it is easy to return to the same old rut.

In many countries there are networks of temporary shelters which offer refuge to battered wives and their dependents. These are not limited to use by local women, though language can occasionally be a problem in some countries. In fact, quite a few shelters suitable for foreign women can be found in many places with an expatriate community, maintained by missionary and other public service organizations. All battered women's shelters have secret addresses, providing a safe and private haven for these women to think through their options and prepare themselves for whatever change they want to make in life. Telephone numbers for such shelters can be found through community advice bureaus, public or private social welfare organizations, churches or temples, or from the medical officer, if there is one, of the nearest consulate. Telephone calls are treated in strictest confidence.

Tolerating abuse is just as destructive as the beating itself. It is important for a battered woman to understand her own behavior so that she doesn't end up repeating history. Parting with an abusive partner will not totally solve the problem. She needs to learn how to be self-reliant, and to rebuild her self-confidence.

MIXED MARRIAGES AND CULTURAL CONFUSION

Of course, not every expatriate marriage consists of two foreigners. Nowadays, with more liberal attitudes toward interracial marriages, especially in western countries, and increasing cosmopolitanism in major capitals and trading centers around the world, mixed marriages no longer carry the stigma they held a few decades ago.

Nevertheless, many myths still remain about marriages between people of different race, nationality or culture. The most common misconception is that mixed marriages are doomed to failure, just because the couple doesn't share a common background. Few studies claim to show any conclusive evidence that mixed marriages, whether intercultural, interracial, or inter-religious, are any more problem-prone than unicultural matches.

In fact, at best, mixed marriages can be even more successful than single-culture families. Cultural differences can actually add spice and stimulation to a relationship. There is always something new to find out about one another, a wider variety of foods and traditions to enrich a family's daily life, and sources of humor in little cultural gaffes.

The lack of common background can also mean that there is a lack of unspoken assumptions about how each other "should" behave, allowing the relationship to be built on a clean slate. However, this is easier said than achieved. The major hazard facing a cross-cultural partnership is when unspoken assumptions do enter the picture. These can run the gamut from racial stereotyping to assuming that one's own way of doing things is either "universal" or "more sensible" than the foreign spouse's way.

Differences not only in culture, but in personal habits, philosophy or diet can grow into conflict. With most married couples who come from varied backgrounds, conflicts are inevitable. For mixed-race marriages, marital issues can sometimes be confused with cultural differences. This is not really a matter of cultural clash, but of lack of communication.

"I'm tired of spending every weekend with your folks," Nick said impatiently. *"Why don't you—"*

"You foreigners just don't understand. Please stop lecturing me," Rosanna jumped in angrily.

Nick sighed. "Here she goes again. A typical Chinese: every time I try to make some suggestions she cuts off the conversation."

Rosanna, age 29, a Malaysian-born Chinese, married Nick, a 37-year-old Caucasian Canadian, just over a year ago. During the first several months things went smoothly, until arguments began to break out. Nick found this hard to accept. As he put it: "I came to Asia to get away from those loud and argumentative women back home."

Nick and Rosanna obviously have different views toward visiting her family. Rosanna considers it her duty and way of showing love to her parents. Yet Nick, who doesn't share the same affection towards them, finds the regular visits quite annoying and interfering with their married life.

Nick has legitimate reasons for wanting to spend more time alone with his wife rather than with in-laws. However, he also ignores the genuine cultural issues in relating to a Chinese family. He fails to understand that Rosanna, being the eldest daughter, has a strong sense of obligation towards her parents.

Nick feels his in-laws have invaded their privacy.

Thinking his wife puts her parents' interests above his, jealousy and resentment fester inside him. He feels he is being pushed aside and he takes this as a personal insult. He questions whether his wife will ever want to be apart from her family. What began as a cultural difference becomes a personal affront.

On the other hand, Rosanna has many reasons for spending time with her elderly parents. However, she ignores the negative impact this has on her relationship with Nick. She expects her husband to respect her "Chinese culture" and disregards his feelings about the visits.

Rosanna considers Nick to be insensitive and uncaring toward her family. She feels hurt and not understood whenever Nick raises an objection about the visits. Such a thing should be above discussion. After all, that is her "Chinese tradition," which her "foreigner" husband must simply accept. Instead of confronting the emotional issue between them, she cites "cultural differences" as a way to defend her stand and to cut off any further discussion.

It is dangerous to immediately label issues that arise in a mixed marriage as cultural differences.

Undeniably, an individual's behavior is affected by their cultural heritage and upbringing. Yet how an individual deals with it is an entirely different matter. In actual fact, cultural differences are not the cause of the problem. The issue is rather one of unrealistic expectations and miscommunication.

In Rosanna and Nick's case, there appear to be both personal and cultural issues involved. Each finds it convenient to confuse the two in trying to get their own way. Nick discounts the importance to Rosanna of filial piety—a cultural issue—and sees only his wife's "stubbornness". Rosanna discounts Nick's need to spend more time alone with his wife—a personal issue—and sees only his "disrespect" for her cultural traditions.

In fact, they are both right and they are both wrong. Rosanna and Nick's problem is purely a personal, not a cultural, one.

After all, when two people are interacting with each other, cultural differences are personal differences. The people involved in this case are not a generic Chinese versus a generic Caucasian; they are two individuals. They need to resolve problems on an interpersonal level.

This is not to say that Rosanna is wrong in citing Chinese family tradition. But it is her personal choice how much to be guided by tradition. At the same time, Nick must respect the importance such an issue has in Rosanna's life.

The first step is to go beyond looking at the issue as a cultural one. Rosanna cannot expect her husband to simply accept her family obligations on the basis of "I'm Chinese, that's my culture, take it or leave it." Similarly, Nick must realize and accept that his wife's family traditions have a powerful effect on her. It would be wise to stop blaming Rosanna's race, culture or family for the problem, otherwise he will only put her on the defensive.

They both need to recognize the issue is not Nick versus Rosanna's family, nor Asian versus Western culture. It is rather Rosanna and Nick together exploring ways to cope with the family's expectations. A positive attitude toward resolving the conflict will draw them closer rather than alienating each other. Rosanna especially has to be clear with her priorities and make a conscious effort to reserve time for her and Nick, even if it means she has to selectively attend her family activities.

By gaining a clearer understanding of the root of their conflict, they will be able to solve the issue of the weekend visits—and other similar disagreements—with far less acrimony and hurt feelings.

Cultural differences do not spell automatic trouble in a marriage. In fact, cross-cultural marriages in general are no more or less at risk than unicultural matches. However, mixed-race couples need to be extra sensitive in identifying the roots of conflict. It can be too tempting to use cultural differences, whether real or imagined, as an excuse for placing blame or cutting off discussion.

Similarly, respect for one's own and one's spouse's cultures is essential in a mixed relationship. However, both sides must be careful not to place too much weight on "culture" or "tradition" in dictating behavior. Remember, when there is a difference of opinion in a relationship, it is individuals in conflict, not races, religions or cultures.

CHILDREN WON'T SAVE AN AILING MARRIAGE

It is not unusual to find expatriate couples having their first, or a new, child within a year after arriving in their overseas post. Usually there are very good reasons for this.

Financial security, often accompanied by the convenience of having a live-in maid, make this an opportune time to have children.

A new baby in the family can make a couple feel closer and stronger at a time when they are far away from family and old friends. But sometimes, particularly among expatriates, children seem to create conflicts between the parents. This is probably because they never asked each other why they wanted a child in the first place.

"He makes me feel that spending time with our son is a crime," Rebecca cried.

Rebecca, 27 years old, is married and has a one-year-old son. She relocated from Belgium to Korea two years ago because of her husband's job.

During a recent argument, her husband William threatened to leave her. He complained that Rebecca focuses all her attention on the child and completely ignores him. Rebecca is hurt and confused, and finally sought therapy.

"Maybe he's right, that I don't have much time for William. But the baby needs my attention and I truly enjoy taking care of him." Rebecca sighed. "All William thinks of is himself."

It is not unusual that new parents are preoccupied with their newborn and spare little time for each other. But if the marriage is stable, eventually the couple will adjust to a more balanced family life without excluding one another.

However, in the case of William and Rebecca, each blames the other for being inconsiderate and uncaring. As far as William is concerned, the baby makes him feel an outsider at home. For Rebecca, her child provides a needed source of love. The baby appears to have created a conflict between them. But this issue is more the symptom than the real problem.

Apparently there was not much communication or affection between William and Rebecca prior to their son's birth. William is very much caught up with his work since moving to Korea. When he comes home, he's usually too tired to talk. Rebecca feels frustrated, lonely and isolated in a foreign country. Though both sense the emotional vacuum they are in, they have allowed it to become the norm in their family. Both thought having a baby would resuscitate their marriage.

In fact, this phenomenon is especially common among expatriate or transient families. Many nonworking wives feel isolated and vulnerable overseas. With husbands absorbed by their work, and with little else to fulfill them in the foreign country, many wives find themselves in need of an outlet: something to absorb them emotionally, as well as to occupy their time. A new-born infant is the perfect and "safe" solution. For husbands, too, a baby is seen as a positive addition to the family, and a source of fulfillment for their wives.

Rebecca finds the baby really has opened a new emotional outlet for her. "I am much happier since my son came," she claims. The child gives her lots of uninhibited affection, something she hasn't experienced for a long time. In return, she draws closer to the baby, showering it with all her love and attention. Such a move pulls her farther away from her husband. Even when William is home, most of Rebecca's attention is given to the baby. In other words, the baby's arrival did not draw the couple closer, but rather drove a further wedge into a problem that was already there.

Many people believe that having children will make a marriage stronger and closer. Having a baby does provide a physical link between a couple but it will not change existing attitudes or feelings between them. In fact, the couple's differences will further intensify when children are involved. Disagreements over child rearing can provide even more fuel for conflicts. In reality, the maxim "kids will make us closer" will work only for a strong and stable marriage.

However, for an unstable marriage, parenthood can make it even weaker.

If a couple's reason for having a child is only to fill an emotional gap—whether in the marriage or within one partner—not only will they be disappointed, but it will also adversely affect the child. One or both parents will unintentionally exert pressure on their child to fulfill the need that their spouse cannot satisfy. Children growing up in such an environment will feel obliged to show greater loyalty to one parent than to the other. Such a demand is devastating to a child's emotional development. It often will lead to guilt feelings as well as self-punishment.

When planning to have a baby, most people focus on their financial readiness and other arrangements of childcare. Unfortunately, many would-be parents don't question themselves about their own emotional readiness or whether their marriage can endure the change of adding a new member to the family.

It is vital for any couple, whether they live overseas or not, to ask themselves, "Why?" before rushing to have children. If the answer is, "to rekindle our marriage," then this is an indication that further questioning is necessary.

Mutual support between new parents not only provides a healthy environment for a child to grow, it will also lead to intimate growth within a marriage. With understanding and love, children can make a good marriage better. However, if one partner is unhappy, or if the marriage is troubled to begin with, no "super" child can make a mediocre marriage flourish.

Time, care and communication

Regardless of the source of their problems, it is essential for any couple to find time to be together and voice their concerns, but without making personal attacks.

If one spouse's so-called "victory" will cause his or her partner pain, or to lose pride, trust or self-esteem, the win actually spells loss on both sides. This can result in losing intimacy or even the marriage.

Disagreements are unavoidable when people live together. But as long as arguments are kept in the open, without hiding behind defenses, consensus and agreement are likely to prevail. The bottom line is, if a couple does care about their marriage it really doesn't matter how busy they are, what backgrounds they come from, or whether they have family or business obligations, they will find time to resolve problems.

Chapter 3

Third culture kids

International children

The internationalization of business has added to the ranks—once the domain of diplomats, missionaries and the military—of a special caste: the international family. This includes families stationed for long periods in a single foreign country and those who relocate every so often to various points around the globe.

These families are producing a new breed of children—Third Culture Kids—who grow up outside their own (or at least their parents') native country. The place their parents refer to as "home" is something thousands of kilometers away, which they may only see for two weeks out of the year. Naturally, a child who grows up in a single country, though it may be "foreign" to his or her parents, will usually think of the place as their real home. But tens of thousands of children around the world experience from Day One that "home" is a place they occupy for two or three years before going on to the next location.

This sort of upbringing is an extraordinary experience for a human being: to grow up as a true "person of the world", familiar with a broad spectrum of languages and cultures, someone who is likely to be open-minded and knowledgeable about our planet and its people. Most international parents can be rightly proud to have given their children such a precious opportunity.

But as with so many good things in life, it comes with sacrifices. Many international children grow up feeling rootless. Add to this that most such children are raised in the rarefied atmosphere of expatriate societies, which are usually very affluent (compared to the surrounding society), elite (top businessmen and diplomats), and insular, socializing mostly among their own small, cliquish group. They attend international schools, enjoy the amenities at their parents' exclusive social and country clubs, take holidays abroad, and receive large weekly allowances.

Thus, international children are usually raised in a country they're told is not their own, within a tiny subset of society comprised of people who are racially, linguistically and culturally different from the surrounding population.

Many complain later that they felt isolated and lonely as children, without long-term friends, and consider themselves to be socially awkward. As adults, they may feel unable to settle down in a single place. Often they feel like social outcasts back in the country their parents call "home". Such people can grow up feeling they don't belong anywhere.

POOR LITTLE RICH KIDS

"Sure, I can show off to friends that I'll have lived around the world before I turn twenty. But what do I get? Nothing. No friends, busy parents and no place I feel is home."

Katy, age 14, relocated to Bangkok with her family about six months ago. Her father's job requires them to move around. Bangkok is the fourth place they have lived in the last six years, after Cairo, Jakarta and Mumbai.

According to her mother, Katy has been depressed, anti-social and withdrawn for the past two months.

During a recent family trip her parents tried to talk with Katy about her feelings, but found it difficult to get their daughter to open up to them. Finally, they sought therapy.

Katy apparently feels hostile towards her parents. She blames them for treating her like merchandise. "They send me here and pay to get me fixed. But they never have time for me or to hear what I have to say," Katy chokes with tears.

After several weeks, her mother was invited to join one therapy session.

"Of course we care about you, Katy," Mom said. "I thought you enjoy your independence. You know your Dad and I are busy and have to do lots of entertaining. We figured you're old enough and don't want to be dragged along to parties. So we give you money to go out with your friends, and we never question your whereabouts. We thought this would show how much we trust and respect you," Katy's mother explained.

"Sure, I have all the money I need so I can go out...and you don't care where I am! At least I won't be in your way and you and Dad don't have to see me or deal with me. I bet you never notice whether I'm there or not," Katy said bitterly.

Clearly there is misunderstanding between mother and daughter. Each tends to see things only from their own perspective. Both feel rejected and unloved.

Adolescence is the time young people begin to find their own identity. Identification with peers is an important part of this process. However, in Katy's case, the frequent relocations deprive her of a stable environment where she can be part of a regular peer group. Each time the family moves, Katy has to start all over again: adjusting to a new environment, new school system and worst of all, to a new group of peers who may or may not accept her. She feels building friendships is a waste of effort because inevitably the family will move again. The risk of rejection has put Katy in a rather defensive state. So, instead of reaching out to friends she turns to her parents for security and comfort.

Without a clear understanding of what she is going through, Katy's parents try to nourish their daughter's sense of independence, with good intentions, by "letting her be on her own". They enjoy living in different parts of the world. They expect Katy to experience the same spirit of adventure. They fail to realize the impact the relocations have on Katy.

Like most parents, they believe children can adapt to new surroundings much faster than adults. Therefore no special effort was made to help Katy adjust, beyond the superficial details of currency, food, and so on. Their social lives and entertaining preoccupy them and leave very little time for Katy.

Feeling alone and uncared for by her parents, Katy reacts with hostility and resentment. Consequently, she retreats within herself.

Katy's case is one of many expatriate children whose families are transient. In such families both the child and parents can experience hurt. Both can feel unloved and unappreciated. Often the problem can be traced to less-than-open communication within the family. The only way to bridge the gap is through direct expression of feelings rather than making assumptions about each other.

Special effort is needed, especially on the parents' part, to help children adjust to a new environment. Giving them time and patience is the first step. Parents need to resist the temptation of offering money to their children instead of time. In most cases, time, love and affection offered by parents can do their children far more good than therapy.

Parents and children should cherish their precious moments as a family. Career, entertaining and travel are all important, but nothing can replace or compensate for those priceless few years of family togetherness before the children grow up and are gone.

WHY EXPATRIATE CHILDREN
SUFFER AT BOARDING SCHOOL

There are many good reasons to send children to the homeland or a third country to attend boarding school. It is often assumed from birth that a child will go. In some circumstances, the host country educational system doesn't suit the needs or requirements of the children. There are so many reasons, in fact, that a great number of parents never stop to think that there may possibly be disadvantages. But unless a child is of the right mind and character, the move could cause lasting psychological damage.

> *"It hurts me to see him so unhappy. But we don't want him to just come home and stop trying. One of these days he has to learn to adapt," Beth said.*

Beth and her husband have lived in Malaysia and Indonesia for over eleven years. Seven months ago they sent their eldest son, Richard, 13, to boarding school in England. They have been informed by the school that their son is anti-social and frequently complains of insomnia, headaches and stomach pains. Richard himself asked to come home shortly after school started.

Since Richard has no previous history of physical or emotional problems, he is most likely reacting to the stress of changes in his life. Richard clearly isn't coping.

Moving to a new environment requires emotional maturity, courage and a willingness to adapt. Though England was his birth place, it hasn't been home for most of his life, so from Richard's point of view he was delivered to a distant foreign country and is likely to feel very alien there. The adjustment that an expatriate teenager has to go through when moving halfway around the world to study is no less than what his parents went through when they moved overseas in the first place. The difference is, the parents did it as fully-mature adults, with their whole family, whereas Richard is doing it alone. Cultural adjustment, homesickness, the pressure of adjusting to the new school, teachers and peers, and overall reluctance to be where he is, could be too much for him to bear.

A child relocating alone faces additional issues. They have to undergo a drastic change of family structure. They must be responsible for their self-care, live in a disciplined institutional setting and learn to rely less on adult support. People at such an age are discovering their self-identity. They like to show off in order to demonstrate their "specialness".

Expatriate children who have broad experience traveling or living in a different culture may hold themselves above their peers or be envied by them. This can slow down their progress in mixing with a new group of friends.

Most parents believe that boarding school offers their child a dose of independence. Thus, much effort is made to find the "right" school and guardian, while less attention is given to the emotional readiness of the child. In fact, independence is a gradual process, which requires guidance, encouragement and time. Regardless of their relationship with their parents, the separation is traumatic.

Often adults make the assumption that children will adapt easily and quickly. Parents sometimes are misled by their child's rapid body growth into thinking they are mature or "adult". However, at Richard's age, not every child has the emotional maturity to endure dramatic change and tolerate stress brought on by leaving the warm family bonds. The adjustment can be more painful than a child may admit to parents, who have loaded him with so many hopes and expectations.

Too often when youngsters are put into situations that they are not ready for they simply mask their fear and insecurity by repressing their emotions. Prematurely pushing adolescents to be independent may conversely result in them having more self-doubt than confidence. All this can have a long-term impact on their mental health and future relationships, which can continue into adulthood.

However, returning him or her to the family is not necessarily the solution. Parents are advised to contact the head teacher directly in order to get a better understanding of the seriousness of the child's distress. Further decisions shouldn't be made until a thorough assessment is done. Parents should use the next holiday or school break to visit their child and encourage him to openly talk about the problems without fear of repercussions or pressure.

Sending an adolescent to boarding school not only impacts the child but the whole family. Sometimes one parent is less committed to the boarding school option, and the separation can adversely affect that parent's life as well. Often one parent may remain for extended periods in the same country where the child attends boarding school in order to support him or her, but also to soothe their own guilt about sending the child away. This can inadvertently cause a rift in the marriage and the family as a whole.

Shirley's two children started boarding school in Britain. She went along for the first three months to help settle them in. Since returning to rejoin her husband she is unable to relax and they have been having many arguments, something which they have not experienced for several years.

Shirley's friends said she and Bill must be going through "Empty Nest Syndrome". Empty Nest Syndrome usually is experienced by couples whose children have reached adulthood and left home, and is discussed later in this chapter. However, it is not Empty Nest Syndrome that Shirley and Bill are dealing with. After all, their children are adolescents and Shirley's role of caring for them is still intact. The only difference is now she has to provide parenting at long distance, which can be difficult to cope with. She feels torn: she sent her young daughters abroad for their benefit, yet she still wants to be with them and maintain the mother-daughter bonds.

Sending a child abroad requires physically letting go. Yet emotionally it can be quite traumatic for many parents. From Shirley's perspective, her staying three months in Britain was for the sake of her girls. However, she doesn't realize she is giving mixed messages to the children. On the one hand, she encourages them to be independent, while on the other hand not trusting them to do so.

Shirley's extended absence causes disruption to her home life as well. It has stirred up conflicts and tension between her and Bill. When he suggested she take it easy and let the girls adjust, she interpreted this to mean he doesn't care about them.

Shirley is in a difficult position. She expects herself to be both mother and wife in two places at once. Without realizing it, she exerts pressure both on herself and the other members of her family.

For example, if Bill doesn't initiate writing letters to the children she concludes he doesn't miss them. He criticizes her for even implying such a thing, which in turn angers her and she starts picking on Bill. The conflicts take on a snowball effect. Meanwhile, when the girls don't constantly mention that they miss her she worries they are losing their closeness as a family.

A parent in Shirley's position needs to set her priorities straight. She hasn't lost her bond with her children by their absence. But she could hurt her marital bonds through her own long absences. She first needs to maintain a stable and happy household with her husband which her children can return to. This means not taking frequent or extended trips alone to visit the children.

Secondly, she has to come to terms with the separation and acknowledge that the parent-child relationship is bound to be different from this point on. It doesn't mean the family will fall apart. But the fact remains that her children will start building new support for themselves without constantly running to Mom.

She also needs to withhold judgment as to how Bill "should" feel in terms of missing the girls. When Bill doesn't openly lament his children's absence, this does not mean he doesn't care.

She must give time for her own adjustment at not having the children around. She shouldn't deny or swallow her sadness over missing her children. But running there is only a short-term way of covering her pain. Inevitably she has to learn to loosen the reins and allow everyone, children included, to adjust to the separation.

Parents need to ask themselves how important it is for them and their children to study abroad. Will the benefits the child may receive outweigh the possible emotional difficulties? Will the parents themselves be able to adjust?

When parents first consider sending their children to boarding school, whether or not it is "family tradition" or has been decided from birth, it should not be presented as a *fait accompli*. It is crucial to look at the child's social, emotional, psychological and mental readiness prior to any decision. Overall, the benefit of education should not override the emotional and psychological security of a child.

If the decision is made to study abroad, children need to be prepared psychologically and emotionally long before the actual move. Parents should create an opportunity to listen to their child's feelings, concerns or worries. Help them to set realistic expectations and teach them ways to manage their concerns. Some basic survival skills and knowledge of how to deal with the stages of acculturation will help a child feel more confident about setting off alone. In short, parents must help their child get used to the idea of being away from their real home and provide them with realistic expectations.

If one or more family members are truly unable to cope with the separation, the decision to send a child overseas should be deferred until these questions can be answered clearly. If they do go ahead with the decision, everyone needs to prepare for the separation and learn to strike a new balance in their family life.

SERVANTS AND SEPARATION

One of the benefits of living in a developing country is that most expatriate families can enjoy the luxury of a live-in maid. Even those couples who put off hiring a servant will do so once a baby is born. In most cases, the helper assumes a major role in child-rearing, inevitably building a close bond. But when an expatriate family relocates, the children are likely to experience the trauma of losing someone near and dear to them.

At a farewell banquet for the Lee family, who return to Australia in three weeks, family photos were passed around. Their only child, Tommy, about three years old, stared at a photo of himself and the family's housemaid with tearful eyes. He pointed repeatedly at the photo of the maid and wept. A family friend turned to pictures of the child standing alone and said: "Look, Tommy! There you are!" But Tommy flipped the pages back to the maid's picture and cried again.

Both parents frowned and looked somewhat annoyed at the child's reaction. Mrs. Lee said, "Don't be silly, she's not even part of the family," as she took the photo album away. She looked at her guests, embarrassed, and shrugged. "The woman hasn't even gone yet and look how he carries on!"

Little Tommy Lee is obviously upset about the impending separation from his nanny. His parents are evidently annoyed by his display of emotion. As friendly as they may be with their maid, she is still clearly a servant. Tommy, however, is unable to make such a distinction. Throughout his entire life she has been his "third parent", with whom he has had frequent intimate contact, who bathed him and changed his diapers.

Obviously the child's outburst triggered some resentment, jealousy and hurt feelings in the parents, who may feel that the child values the maid more than them. They may subconsciously deny the fact that Tommy's separation from a servant could cause him pain.

For Tommy this is probably the first major loss in his young life. Such an experience is anxiety-provoking. The commonly-held notion that young children can't understand what is going on is completely false. Although only three, Tommy has advanced cognitive skills and is aware of what is happening with the separation. But with his still limited language ability, the only way he can express his fears is through crying and disturbances in his eating, sleeping, and elimination.

On top of this, soon he will find himself in a totally new environment. After the move the whole family must readjust to life without a house servant. Both parents will be more involved in housekeeping chores, making them less energetic or available for the child in terms of play and fun. The parents will therefore be likely to impose more rules and restrictions on the child. Tommy will also need to relearn certain verbal and non-verbal signs and signals from his parents which could be quite different from those he learned earlier from the maid. In other words, both Tommy and his parents will be under some stress because of the move and the family's restructuring itself without a live-in maid.

Naturally, if the family plans to hire a nanny in the new location, the situation is different, but only by a small degree. The fact of severed bonds with a cherished adult remains. So many changes happening within a short period will create a rather traumatic experience for Tommy. Parents in similar situations should not overlook the seriousness of what the child is going through.

Families preparing to relocate may be preoccupied with the business of moving, farewell parties, and so on. Parents may be tempted to leave their children with the maid even more often than before, up until the date of actual departure.

This is probably the worst thing they could do for the child's mental health. A smooth transition during the adjustment period is essential. It is crucial for the parents to spend more time with their children long before the actual departure. If he or she has others to fall back on, the anxieties will be less intense when separated from the maid.

Ideally, it would be best for the maid to be phased out gradually so that the child can adjust to the change slowly and at the same time build a closer bond with the parents. She would spend only a few days a week with the child during the last three months and then gradually cut this down as the time of departure approaches. However, this may not be practical for most families.

Try to use the child's language or games to illustrate the move and the maid's leaving, so as to provide a chance for him or her to rehearse the separation. Parents must also acknowledge and deal with their own hidden resentment toward their child's attachment to the maid. Lastly, parents should expect a period of bereavement during which the child cries more, has trouble sleeping and eating, and wets the bed. If patient care and sensitivity are given to the child during the adjustment period, he or she will gradually get over the trauma and anxiety as time goes by.

SHARED CUSTODY:
INTERNATIONAL TUG-OF-WAR

Separation from any close adult is hard on a child. But when one parent goes away, perhaps separated by thousands of kilometers, a child's life can be torn apart.

"How can I trust him anymore? He abandoned us and left Mom so unhappy," Martha cried.

Martha, age 12, moved back to Canada with her mother about a year ago, after her parents' divorce. She recently returned to Hong Kong for two months during the school break at the request of her father.

Bill frowned. "I thought you wanted to spend some time with me. Instead you treat me like a stranger."

"What about you? You moved out just like that. You think you treat us any better?" Martha broke into tears.

After breaking off his 17-year marriage, Bill wants to maintain a good relationship toward his daughter, with whom he used to be very close. However, upon Martha's arrival Bill finds her unapproachable. She puts up a cold front toward him. Every time Bill wants to talk to her she turns quiet. She appeared especially rude and inconsiderate when they went out with Bill's girlfriend. Bill realizes no matter how many concessions he makes, his daughter will not let him in. He has become quite disturbed.

Martha's way of responding to her father is rather common among children from divorced families. She is wary of getting too close to the person who, in her mind, abandoned her and the family. The only way she can express her anger and insecurity is by closing herself off and protesting with silence.

Even though her father explained that the divorce was a mutual decision, Martha sees it as a case of her father walking out on her mother. She resents her father for disrupting the family peace. The fact that he has a new girlfriend and an orderly life, while mother is all alone, reinforces this belief.

Like many children from broken homes, she takes the side of the parent—her mother—who appears to be the victim of the other's action. She feels that if she gets close to her father again it will be seen as giving approval to him divorcing her mother.

Often children in a divorced family will assume the role of the missing spouse. Martha feels responsible for providing comfort and support to her mother. Yet her own feelings about the family splitting up have to be swallowed. "Mother is too busy being angry. She just doesn't understand how I feel," Martha said. However, she sees Father seemingly adjusting well and living a new life with another woman. He is having it easy while she and her mother are still struggling with the after-effects. All this creates bitterness in her.

Most children have a difficult time accepting that divorce is final. They often harbor fantasies that Mom and Dad will somehow reunite and the family will be restored. Whenever possible, they try to mention favorable things about one parent in front of the other, in the hope that one day they can draw their parents back together. But seeing her father and his new girlfriend has destroyed Martha's fantasy. Feelings of jealousy and hopelessness finally set in when she realizes the divorce is irreversible.

Terminating a marriage involves a lot of tearing and restructuring. Couples are usually preoccupied with their own feelings and trying to survive such a drastic change. Sometimes children's needs are unintentionally ignored. Seldom are they given a chance to express their feelings towards the parents' separation. They may be caught in a tug-of-war or be called on to take sides.

Children from expatriate families experience additional adverse effects when their parents divorce. In many cases, when a couple gets divorced, one partner may lose the legal right to remain in the foreign land. Others by choice choose to return to their home country. In either case, children can be a continent apart from their non-custodial parent. Not only do they experience the split-up of their family, but also a long-distance separation from one parent. Weekend visits are impossible, and telephone contact is prohibitively expensive. Such a setup creates a damper in maintaining the stable parent-child relationship which a child needs in the process of growing up.

Divorce for an expatriate child means losing more than a parent. If they are in the custody of the repatriating parent, they then lose school, friends, and the country they grew up in and consider home. This can lead to resentment and bitterness. Without opportunity to clarify their confusion, children will draw their own conclusions over who "really" caused a divorce. Furthermore, without a channel to voice their feelings, they inevitably feel alienated from one or both parents. This leads to frustration and feelings of helplessness. It will also have a negative impact on how they treat or view other relationships in the future.

In helping children to deal with divorce, parents must share with them what is happening in order to avoid any misconceptions. Reassure children that they are not responsible for breaking up the marriage, and that it is entirely the adults' decision. It is important to point out that even though the parents no longer live together, both will continue to love and care for the children.

Avoid lying for the sake of "protecting the children's feelings". Unless children are given clear information, they will form their own conclusions, which may be incorrect. Given the real facts, they are less likely to entertain any false hopes of parental reunion. They are also more unlikely to take sides, or to favor one parent over the other.

Finally, children ought to be given opportunities to voice their feelings, ideally before the divorce, so that all parties can have a better understanding of others' reactions and try to work it through in the best way they can.

The Empty Nest

Children do grow up and most leave home. Expatriate parents especially will feel the pain of separation when their children are thousands of kilometers and oceans apart. This is a difficult time of adjustment for parents, when two people may have to get to know each other all over again.

> *"I was never happy for the last twenty years," Gaby said in an angry tone.*
>
> *Herbert scowled and appeared shocked to hear his wife's statement.*

Both Gaby and Herbert are in their mid-forties, married 24 years and have two children. They have lived in the Middle East and Far East for nearly twenty years. Their son moved back to Switzerland last year and their daughter left six months ago for Germany to attend university.

Gaby has been feeling agitated and depressed. She complains that Herbert never has any time for her. Last month they finally took a 10-day vacation together. She returned feeling even more unhappy. "On the outside we seemed to be having a good time on our holiday, but in fact we had nothing to say or share with each other. I feel even more lonely being with him." It was then that she sought counseling. After a few sessions, the therapist requested that Herbert accompany her for one session.

> *"Our children kept us close but they also kept us busy. I thought that when they'd gone, Herbert and I would enjoy each other more, but he doesn't seem to care about me," Gaby complained.*

Gaby is going through what many mothers go through at this stage: the Empty Nest Syndrome. She quit her job when they left Switzerland twenty years ago, and devoted her time to the family and children. Child rearing became her top priority. With the children gone, she finds herself all alone during the day, no longer busy cleaning up after the kids or having the pleasure of conversing with them as young adults. Naturally, she turns to Herbert and hopes he can help fill the gap in her life. Yet, to her surprise and dismay, she finds that she seems hardly to know him anymore.

In most families, children unavoidably distract parents' attention from each other. Dealing with kids may help the adults feel closer, especially when mutual support is needed in discipline during the rebellious adolescent years. But children can also help parents divert or delay marital conflicts by focusing most of their conversation on the children instead of each other. This is a convenient way of avoiding conflict temporarily, but when unspoken tension is prolonged, couples can grow apart without realizing it. When their children are gone, all these differences or unnoticed problems will inevitably return.

Empty Nest Syndrome can have a great impact on an expatriate family. The fact is, many of these children do not simply move out of the home, but end up a continent away from their parents. This makes it even more difficult for many parents to deal with.

A large number of expatriate families send their children overseas or "back home" to boarding school. When they go off to university, the chances are quite high that they will attend a school abroad rather than in their parents' vicinity. Therefore, the age expatriate children leave home is generally younger. In turn, expatriate parents experience the Empty Nest sooner.

At the same time, many expatriates travel frequently for work. Their children keep the home-based spouse—usually the wife—company and therefore are the ones holding the family intact. When children are gone it can be a devastating blow for the family, especially the wife. The loneliness of the husband's frequent travel, which may previously have been eased by having the children around, may become unbearable. Many of these wives now desperately want to get closer to their husband.

According to both Gaby and Herbert, they have had a fairly good marriage. Gaby's complaint that the last twenty years were total misery is very much her projection of present dissatisfaction. Undoubtedly, though, they have been having some differences and problems which were either ignored or denied by both of them.

> *"She is getting very difficult to please," Herbert said. "She complains that I never go out with her to cultural events, so I went along with her last week to a ballet performance. But she yelled at me afterward and said I didn't appreciate it." Herbert shrugged with exasperation.*

Herbert is also adjusting to a family without children around. The children have always provided a comfortable distance between him and Gaby. In coping with Gaby's yearning for closeness, and his being more comfortable at a distance, he works more late hours and sometimes even brings work home. The more Herbert avoids close contact, the more insecure and unwanted Gaby feels. Mistrust and resentment started building up, which put an even wider gap between them.

For a family to keep equilibrium each member needs to maintain a certain role. Once the children leave home most couples are forced to relate to each other in a different way in order to strike a new balance. Presumably, after many years of marriage they would expect to have a very intimate partner. Yet when closer contact is made he or she realizes the spouse is a semi-stranger.

"Children can make a married couple closer" is really a myth. If there are flaws in the marriage, no child can solve them. Having children may temporarily remove the symptoms, even for twenty years, but the problems remain.

Without a doubt, child rearing is time-consuming, as well as rewarding. But it is also important for married couples to reserve time for intimacy and not put it aside until they have spare time. The spare time may not come until twenty years later. Maybe by then, nothing will be able to bridge the gaps and differences that have built up over many years.

Parents and children

Living overseas is quite a different experience for children than it is for their parents. Their view of moving abroad can be quite at odds with that of adults. Those actually born outside the "home" country consider the itinerant life to be the norm.

When they're grown up and gone, parents should remind themselves that their progeny are only repeating what they themselves did by moving to another country in the first place.

Enjoy the precious time together while you have it. Then every member of the family can share in the advantages of a lifestyle that few people on this earth will ever have the good fortune to experience.

Chapter 4

Stress at work and home

COMING TO TERMS WITH STRESS

STRESS IS ONE of the most talked-about phenomena of the modern world. Almost every day one is likely to see a new article or miracle treatment for this 21st Century epidemic. Stress is blamed for physical ailments, such as ulcers and heart attacks, psychosomatic problems, such as insomnia and headaches, and psychological disturbances, like depression. Careers falter, marriages break up, and hair turns prematurely gray, all on account of stress. And nowhere is stress to be found more than in the highly-strung, high-rolling, on-the-go world of expatriates.

It is easy to blame the increasingly high-tech environment, fast pace and competitiveness of the contemporary urban lifestyle, as well as the special pressures of living overseas, for causing stress. No doubt the environment does contribute to the stress one experiences. However, not every person will become stressed in the same anxiety-provoking situation. The fact is, some people are more prone to stress than others. This has a lot to do with an individual's personality, self-esteem and past experiences.

> "My lower back pain is killing me. I know my work is not up to my normal standard, but I can't help it. I hate the way my boss lectures me as if I'm an idiot," David said with visible anger.

David, 27 years old, is a senior artist in a foreign branch of an international public relations firm. It is a responsible, challenging position and his first overseas posting. Two months ago he started experiencing insomnia and hypertension. Naturally, he concluded these were caused by the stress of overwork. Soon after, he developed severe lower back pain and stomach cramps, which made working intolerable. As he watched the quality of his work decline, he began to feel even more stressed.

David has been through various treatments, from prescribed drugs to weekly massages. The symptoms subside for a short while, then the pain returns.

Stress is a response to perceived helplessness and lack of control over a specific problem or situation. It is not a physical problem, but rather a physical manifestation. Stress is not caused only by the external environment or lifestyle, but also by the unresolved conflicts within a person. Therefore, what most people call "stress" is not really a disease or disorder that can be treated directly. It is a symptom with its cause varying from one person to the next.

In David's case, instead of blaming his problem on stress, he needs to examine why he has stress in the first place. After looking into his background, it became clear that he felt guilty for pursuing art rather than business, as well as moving far away from home, both against his parents' wishes. Without realizing it, he was constantly trying to regain their trust and respect through career accomplishments. Meanwhile, at work his talent is very much treated as a mere commercial accessory, and receives little appreciation. He resents being in such a position. However, quitting the job would be a sign of failure and would reinforce his parents' notion of his having made the wrong career choice in the first place. He escapes his dilemma by getting sick, and thus avoiding work.

When a person cannot directly deal with stress, he or she may unconsciously convert it into a physical disability or psychosomatic illness, such as ulcers, bladder control problems, acne, obesity, neck pain or asthma. The disability then diverts attention from the situation that created stress in the first place. The individual usually cannot see the relationship between the sickness and the cause of it.

Stress is almost unavoidable in our daily life. In fact, stress can be beneficial in limited doses. It can stimulate the senses and help one get things done more efficiently. However, if a person is constantly under stress it can be quite damaging to mental and physical health.

There is no one magic treatment for stress. For many people symptomatic treatment is likely to be sufficient. Relaxation exercises and various forms of meditation and massage will help remove the block and put the person back in focus, enabling him or her to carry on with life.

But some people are incapacitated by stress at work or home. If a person feels mentally overwhelmed, accident-prone or violent, it indicates that the problem is more deep-seated.

Some people run to psychiatrists for medication in order to chemically regulate their stress. In certain cases, drugs may be appropriate, though they pose the danger of psychological or physical dependency. For most, medication won't help the underlying conflicts, which are caused by psychological factors which need to be confronted directly. In such cases, long-term treatment in psychotherapy will help unveil the underlying issues in their life, enabling them to see why they react so negatively to stressful situations.

Stress is not a general condition, but an individual problem, depending on a person's mental and physical health and level of tolerance. Increasing basic self-awareness of your own limits, and learning not to over-extend yourself, will enable most of us to cope in a highly-strung modern society.

EXECUTIVE HYPOCHONDRIA

No group is more prone to stress than business executives. Look in their desk drawers and you are likely to find an assortment of pharmaceuticals, headache tablets, stomach pills, asthma inhalers, and muscular pain ointments.

The higher one rises through the ranks, the more decisions have to be made alone: an enormous responsibility for any person. Many expatriate business people were middle-ranking officials in their home offices, sent to assume elevated positions in the overseas branch. The sudden rise in status and responsibility can be an enormous shock.

Again, it is tempting to blame the job itself, and the environment, for causing stress. Most people consider stress and its related problems as "part of the job". In fact, this avoids the issue. In reality, stress, its causes and its cure are an internal matter.

"My ulcer is a professional hazard," Tom said. "They say I'm too hard on myself. But people just don't understand the responsibilities I have!"

Tom, 41, an expatriate business executive, is perceived by his peers as successful and hard-working. However, he doesn't view himself as successful and constantly worries that failure will be around the corner. He finds himself unable to sit back and relax. He continuously does things to make sure his projects or business deals won't fall through.

"I don't mind working hard, but deep inside I don't feel happy," Tom explained.

Tom is a hard-driving character who sets high goals and drives himself and others in order to achieve them. The inspiration behind his work initiative is his chronic concern that he will not reach his goals or that he or his subordinates will make costly errors. Such worries make him doubt his abilities and cause him a great deal of distress.

Whenever he is under pressure his ulcer acts up. Several times he has had to go to hospital in the middle of a business deal. He is exasperated and upset that both his capabilities and physical health are letting him down. Tom's reaction is to push himself even harder.

It is easy to blame the stress of the job and of the place for Tom's ulcer. But many of the problems that people blame on stress are not necessarily caused by the environment. Stress in fact can be generated internally. For example, Tom finds it difficult to delegate tasks because all he can think of is how everything might go wrong. Even if he delegates the work, he keeps the stress.

What Tom is battling is more than his workload and physical condition: he is wrestling with psychosomatic illness. Psychosomatic illness is a psychological condition which manifests itself as physical illnesses. Through their physical sickness people can avoid, delay or distract themselves from unpleasant predicaments. Sometimes people may find a certain situation too frightening or too painful to deal with and getting sick can allow them to escape from the confrontation. This process usually does not proceed consciously. For example, a woman finds it painful to meet with her ex-husband. Whenever she is required to attend such a meeting she is struck with a severe migraine headache which prevents her from going.

For some people, psychosomatic illness can help attract the attention they have been longing for. For others, it allows them to feel sorry for themselves, further confirming their feeling of helplessness or incapability. For example, Tom has never believed himself to be a successful person. When he has a chance to prove himself during a business deal, his ulcer forces him to drop out. This reinforces his deep-seated belief that he is a failure.

Psychosomatic illness is also an indication of suppressed fear, frustration or anger. People who are anxiety-prone, or chronic worriers, are more vulnerable to such a disorder. They usually place unrealistic demands on themselves, build up lists of irrational thoughts, and focus their attention on fears of inadequate performance or disaster. They often exaggerate the importance and difficulty of a task and underestimate their capacity to deal with it. In order to avoid the feared confrontation they get ill.

Psychosomatic illness is not easily identified. Some common symptoms are gastric ulcers, tension headaches, asthma, acne or vomiting. Not to say that every one of these physical reactions is psychosomatic. But if some of these symptoms happen regularly under stressful circumstances, during confrontations or when meeting people one wants to avoid, then it is worthwhile to take note of such patterns.

Though psychosomatic disorders are caused by emotional factors, they are real illnesses. People can die even from psychologically-triggered asthma or ulcers. It is important not to dismiss a condition as "merely" psychosomatic and ignore the real physical illness.

Someone in Tom's situation needs to deal with the ulcer right away to make sure no permanent damage is done. Immediate steps to take include: to stop being so self-critical, to delegate work and to accept his own limitations. Meanwhile, he needs to deal with the underlying cause of the psychosomatic illness and understand what function it serves for him.

Psychosomatic illness is harmful and destructive to both the sufferer and their loved ones. Usually such a problem is deep-seated and beyond a person's own awareness. As such, professional psychological help is recommended for people whose life is hindered or threatened by this disorder.

THE EFFECTS OF OVERWORK
ON THE FAMILY

Stress easily spills over into family life. Besides the obvious effects of bringing problems home from work, there is the less-obvious stress on a family caused by a hard-working spouse or parent.

> *"I'm doing it for you and our son, can't you understand? I promise it won't last forever," Peter said.*

> *"Oh yeah?" Joan replied in an angry tone. "How many times have you promised me to cut down your work? I can't stand it anymore!"*

This is one of the arguments Peter and Joan go through every few months. Joan has been threatening to leave Peter unless he does something about his work.

Peter is in his early thirties. He and Joan have been married six years and have a three-year-old son. He was a middle-ranking officer in his management company back in England. Peter was transferred overseas four years ago, for a two-year posting, which he renewed at the end of his contract. Presently Peter is one of the top executives in his local branch office.

Both Joan and Peter were happy to arrive in their foreign posting. Even though the new job demanded more time and energy, Peter was full of enthusiasm to meet new responsibilities and challenges. Joan was very encouraging, as she realized that it was a step up the career ladder for Peter. For her it was a nice change of lifestyle which provided much variety.

By nature Peter is not a workaholic. However, he soon found himself absorbed by his duties as an executive. He stays after work to try to catch up, always promising himself and Joan to return to a normal work schedule "after this project is over." Invariably, a new, urgent project always comes up.

He constantly struggles to strike a balance between work and family. He finds that work always has clear tasks and deadlines, whereas his wife and child don't have any definable problems which require his urgent care. Without realizing it, he yields the first priority to the job's demands, choosing to resolve them before turning attention to the family.

In the beginning Joan was understanding. She kept a positive attitude because she realized that Peter worked for the sake of the family. She tried to remain cheerful and sympathetic when he was too exhausted to talk with her or spend time with their son after work. Slowly Joan's frustration started piling up, but she remained silent in order not to burden Peter.

Peter is aware that his overwork has caused some frustration for his wife. He feels guilty for not being able to spend as much time with the family as he wishes. He keeps reminding himself and Joan that it is only a short-term trade-off. "I'll only work like this for a few years to save up some money. By the time we return home we'll have a better life there," he explains. With such an idea in mind, Peter gradually lets himself get sucked deeper into his work.

When Peter was about to renew a third two-year contract, Joan's patience finally ran out. All her anger and frustration burst forth together. She felt betrayed and taken for granted. She blamed Peter for being insensitive and using the excuse of "the family good" to fulfill his own ambition and desires. By the time the argument erupted their marriage was on the verge of breaking up.

It is rather tragic that a marriage has to come to such a stage. Ironically, Peter feels he is overworking for the good of the family, while Joan feels she is remaining silent about her frustration for Peter's good. Obviously they care for each other. But they make assumptions about what is good for the other and intentionally avoid conflicts. "Trying to do what's best for the other" is actually killing the marriage.

Couples in a similar situation need to confront the real issues. Working spouses need to prioritize their lives and make a clear division between work and family life. When off-duty, begin by turning off the cell phone, computer, and other networked and electronic distractions, to be exclusively with the family.

The other spouse needs to voice her or his feelings and not let things build. Otherwise, unresolved resentments will eventually leak out which can be even more damaging to the marriage. Open communication—the most vital ingredient in any relationship—will not only help resolve conflicts such as Peter and Joan's, but prevent them from arising in the first place.

COPING WITH JEALOUSY

Hard work, responsibility, and a fast-paced environment are not the only factors that contribute to stress. Jealousy, too, which in mild doses can inspire a person to higher achievement, if allowed to fester, will eat up a person inside.

Expatriate society, with its small, close-knit numbers, and its top-heavy professional and economic mix, provides a breeding ground for jealousy. Those foreign residents who don't fit the stereotype of the "glamorous expat lifestyle" are likely to be reminded of this day in and day out by others and themselves.

"It doesn't seem fair. I work hard for my school and students and see what I get." Gary, 29 years old, pounded his fist on the desk.

"Look at Bill: no talent, but gets all the things you and I ever wanted...fat salary, free luxury housing, car..."

Gary moved to Hong Kong 18 months ago for change and adventure. But lately he has been feeling increasingly dissatisfied, unappreciated and unmotivated. He is tempted to quit his teaching job and move back to New Zealand. He is having a hard time facing himself and suffers from insomnia.

He says that he has become extremely conscious of his social status in Hong Kong. Back home Gary rarely mingled with well-off executives. But here among the small expatriate population he finds a limited social environment. Most of the other foreigners he meets are business people, lawyers, or investment bankers, all receiving healthy salaries and perks, their housing paid for. Conversations typically center around real estate or travel to exotic resorts.

Of course, Gary has some local acquaintances, too. But it's only natural for a person to compare her or himself with others in the group to which she or he most belongs—that is, the expatriate community.

At the beginning he convinced himself that he does have a comfortable life in Hong Kong and he didn't come here expecting to get rich. But more and more he finds himself bombarded by the idea of measuring success in terms of wealth. They travel to 5-star Bali resorts at company expense; he takes budget holidays in Thailand. He rides the bus; they have chauffeurs. Unavoidably, he compares himself with his expatriate neighbors and envies the fancy, high-class lifestyle many of them have.

The growing jealousy causes him to feel more and more discontent. He often returns from parties feeling depressed and resentful, so increasingly he shies away from social gatherings. He finds that being with other foreigners reminds him of his "class" and reinforces his feeling of "failure". Inside, he is experiencing tremendous struggle.

On the one hand, he realizes that he wouldn't want to change his job merely to pursue higher income. He knows this is the profession he likes. in which he spent many years earning his credentials. Giving it up is really out of the question. But on the other hand, he cannot control his burning envy. Intellectually, he understands that he shouldn't be feeling this way because he is doing much better abroad than back in New Zealand. Yet the jealousy seems out of his control. His turmoil causes him to feel restless and withdrawn and he is unable to concentrate on his work.

Everyone experiences covetous feelings from time to time. In a society like Hong Kong where success is measured by accumulated wealth, you can easily feel like a loser if you don't score high on the materialist scale. Such feelings are further magnified in expatriate circles, where high salaries and luxury living are the perceived norm.

Coveting can easily turn into an addiction for many people and force them to depend on tomorrow to bring them the happiness that today couldn't supply. The more people measure their significance by bank balances and other people's accomplishments, the less they will be able to feel at ease in their daily lives.

Jealousy is not easy for anyone to handle. Gary's feelings in fact are normal and almost unavoidable, considering the Hong Kong (and particularly the expatriate) lifestyle. However, the mere fact that he left home in New Zealand to move far away overseas could be an indication of underlying dissatisfaction within himself in the first place. Thus, for Gary moving back home will not solve his problem. It would be even more devastating for him to later find out that he can run away from the place, yet he cannot run away from himself.

Gary can eliminate the social class gap by making a conscious effort to expand his circle beyond wealthy expatriates. People of a similar economic level to his own would likely be more accepting and more sensitive to his feelings and needs. There are many clubs and organizations in any country, such as sports, hiking, or special interest groups, which have a variety of members from all races and socioeconomic backgrounds.

Gary needs to get a better understanding of himself. He must identify whether his jealous feelings are situational—caused by economic class difference—or from basic dissatisfaction inside himself. Learning more about himself and his own soft spots will eventually help him to adjust to the peculiar world of expatriate society.

When you just want to give up and go

As we have seen, it is internal factors, rather than the external environment or job, which determine how a person reacts to stress. However, many people will fall victim to stress-related problems in a foreign environment to a degree never suffered back home.

This often leads to a peculiar form of homesickness, in which a person fantasizes that "if only I move back home, to a familiar environment, I'll find relief." Usually, when someone is in such a mood, moving back home is the worst thing he or she could possibly do.

"I'm too young to retire and too old to start all over again back home. I feel stuck here," Gerard said.

Gerard, 47, has been with the Beijing branch of his company for four years. Both he and his family feel quite settled there. On and off he complains about the poor quality of life, the pollution, corruption, pushiness of people and so on. But like most people there, he learned to live with these. Yet for the last six months Gerard has been getting extremely irritated by every little thing. He also feels more and more overwhelmed by his work. His performance has declined, which means he has to spend more time in the office to catch up. This leaves him less time to relax or be with his family. The more exhausted and depressed he becomes, the less work he gets done and eventually he must stay even later and on weekends to catch up. It turns into a vicious cycle.

Gerard threw up his arms. "What do I get out of life in China? I just want to get out of here now."

He claims he wants to drop everything and take the family back to France. But in the back of his mind he knows that at 47 it would not be easy for him to find another good position. "And anyway, I don't know whether I really want to move back home."

Gerard is experiencing "burnout". Burnout is a common term for an extreme form of stress, which occurs when pressures build up and are left untreated over a long period. He feels mentally and physically exhausted and that he has reached his limit. A person may feel fatigued, withdrawn, unmotivated, short-tempered, cynical, easily irritated, and depressed. Even recreation becomes difficult, as he may have lost all enthusiasm for life.

Gerard blames his job and the environment and ignores the real causes of his exhaustion. Burnout is caused not from without but from within. Usually it originates from a general feeling of incessant routine with no end in sight. Feeling that life is one unending series of responsibilities, with no time for oneself and little enthusiasm for anything else, a person easily feels overwhelmed and trapped. Prolonged burnout can damage a person's mental health.

Moving away will not remove burnout. In fact, it is unwise to make any drastic decisions because people usually cannot view things objectively in this state of mind. Gerard is likely thinking of Paris as a haven. Naturally, he will focus on the good things there and totally forget things that might have annoyed him in the past. With such notions in mind, relocation might turn out to be a big disappointment and disaster.

The only lasting cure for burnout is a change in attitude and lifestyle. The first step is to tackle the feeling of being trapped, by altering the routine, removing some of the obvious stresses and actively making the present situation more tolerable. This can include: cutting down outside business meetings, delegating duties to trusted personnel, limiting phone intakes, getting more sleep and not forgetting to give oneself a treat occasionally. This way, the person can regain a sense of control over the situation.

Breaking the routine is essential to tackle burnout. It would be helpful to take a vacation as soon as possible, to refresh both body and mind and regain a sense of balance. However, this is easier said than done for many people. It often takes a concerted effort to pull yourself away from work or duty. A holiday may not be beneficial for the job in the short run, but it will definitely be beneficial for your mental health and performance in the long run.

In Gerard's case, leaving China may be one of many options for change. But instead of immediately rushing into such a major decision, it is advisable to explore first. Taking a brief trip home will give him and the family a more realistic idea of the advantages and disadvantages of relocating.

Burnout is a signal that something needs attention. Avoiding dealing with it may damage your mental health. Obviously, running away will not resolve it either.

THE GREATEST STRESS OF ALL

Even more stressful than burnout on the job is losing a job. This can be especially disorienting for an expatriate who, because of recession and cutbacks back in the home head-quarters, suddenly finds him or herself "retrenched" and unemployed.

What to do then? Where there may have been no tempta-tion up until that point to return to the home country, sud-denly that becomes an option to be weighed against staying put in the foreign country.

Finding a new position takes time, particularly higher positions, and even more so for people in or approaching middle age. Scouting for openings, networking, sending out resumes, waiting for interviews and then responses, can occupy several months. For an expatriate this requires more than mere patience. He or she must constantly grapple with the question: "When do I just give up and go home?"

Irene was recently let go from her position as a marketing executive after twelve years with the company in Thailand.

"I was optimistic to begin with, but after two months' searching, I start wondering whether I'm better off moving back to Australia," Irene said.

A job is relatively easy to replace compared with the confidence which is lost as a result of unemployment. The thought of being out there competing with younger people for jobs is frightening. Suddenly Irene feels old, tired and depressed. People in such a position can easily lapse into a real crisis unless they are aware of what is happening to them.

While awaiting the end of unemployment, it is easy to panic and grasp hold of things or ideas without thorough thought or focus. According to Irene, she's had a business idea for years but never had time to pursue it. She thinks this may be the right time. She's also considering going to school to obtain new credentials which may make her more marketable in the long run. At the same time she is looking into grants for the book she's wanted to write. Meanwhile, she is still supposedly looking for a job. Each of these goals would perhaps have a chance if Irene would concentrate seriously on one task. But dissipating her energy down too many paths at once like this is a recipe for multiple failures.

Amidst all the panic and confusion, the idea of moving back home can be quite appealing. After all, home should be a familiar place which offers hope and relief from the unpleasantness of unemployment overseas. However, "home" is not necessarily home anymore. The fact is, she hasn't spent the last ten-plus years there. She'd have to treat herself like a newcomer to relearn the system and readjust to Australia. This is feasible when one has the time and presence of mind to do so. But for Irene, being unemployed puts her in a very fragile, vulnerable state of mind. Being a stranger in her own land will only compound her anxiety, not relieve it.

Yet she does go back, for weeks at a time. Never long enough to engage in serious job-hunting in Australia, but long enough to nullify her chances in Thailand. Her trips, she explains, are to "give herself time to sort things out," be with friends and family who could provide moral support and to research the job market back home. After all, she says, "nothing is really happening in Bangkok." By running back and forth she decreases her chances of being contacted or interviewed, and of learning about new openings. The situation becomes a vicious cycle: the longer she stays away, the lower the possibility of re-establishing herself in the job market. Irene is in fact sabotaging herself.

Self-sabotage is not a conscious act. Like procrastination on a grand scale, it is a way of avoiding responsibility. Another common way that people in Irene's position sabotage themselves is the unwillingness to accept a position in any way lower than the one previously held. In her mind she holds onto what she used to have and refuses to accept the uncomfortable fact that she may have to take one or two steps backward in order to get on track again. Thus she is closing off opportunities no matter where she goes.

Anyone in Irene's position must do one thing before continuing the job search: decide. Decide where to concentrate efforts (Thailand or Australia), what to concentrate on (job search, business or book), and what is realistically acceptable.

Thailand has been Irene's de facto home for many years. She knows the system and her contacts are there. Her attitude of "maybe I'll go back to Australia" distracts her from committing all her energy into job searching in Thailand. It is advisable to set a realistic time frame on the search in Thailand: for instance, six months. Within that given time she should not allow herself to try halfheartedly, thereby giving herself a reason to leave.

If she chooses to return home after exhausting all resources, it is likewise essential to clarify this decision in her mind: be committed to returning to Australia, and not indulge in thoughts of rushing right back to Thailand or another country if the going gets rough back home.

She also needs to be willing to lower her standard of acceptable jobs. Being offered a lesser-paid position may hurt her ego now, but remaining unemployed and unproductive would be much worse in the long run.

Focusing on one set of goals and priorities is the essential first step toward combating stress, whether that stress comes from job-family conflict, jealousy, burnout or unemployment. It is important to deal with stress where it originates: from within. Otherwise, whether you move, or change jobs, or take medications, you will fall back into the same old patterns. If you are willing to confront your problems with care, it is likely you can work it through and grow from the experience.

Chapter 5

All alone and far from home

LONELINESS

"It's easy to meet people in this town, but so hard to make friends."

An often-thought, sometimes spoken, complaint among people in a foreign land.

Loneliness is the silent plague among expatriate communities around the world. Again, the problem of "identity inflation" (discussed in Chapter Two) creates an illusion of gaiety and romance of life overseas. With all the travel, all the money, all the interesting people to meet...who could have anything to complain about?

People might hint at the problem, but few will admit to actually feeling lonely. Word spreads fast in a small, gossip-mad expatriate community, and everyone is ever-conscious of their personal or business reputation. Admitting to loneliness is admitting to failure.

Loneliness affects every level of expatriate society, from powerful, self-confident business leaders to the many teachers and backpackers who drift from place to place. These can be broken down into four main categories: The Lonely Housewife, The Drifter, The Lonely Working Woman, and The Lonely Working Man. Lonely housewives are looked at in detail elsewhere in this book. In this chapter, we will review the other three types.

THE DRIFTER

"Is it me or is it Singapore?" Rosemary asked.

"All I want is someone to love me and have a family with me. But I seem to always find the wrong men."

Rosemary, age 32, has been in Singapore for three years. She left Boston at age 20 and has been living and working in different parts of the world. She blames the narrow expatriate social circle for limiting her chances of finding the "right" person. She claims that she always ends up hanging around with the same old crowd.

Many people in Rosemary's situation blame expatriate society for their social unfulfillment. It's true that most expatriates have a small social circle, often restricted to people of the same nationality within the same profession. Under such circumstances, the choice of potential partners for a single person is undeniably limited.

Although the situation may place obstacles in a single person's social life, it is not the cause of social unfulfillment. Expat society is likely only one contributing factor, as well as a convenient excuse.

According to Rosemary, everywhere she goes she keeps entering unhealthy relationships and ends up being taken advantage of or exploited. Likewise, apparently good relationships often fall apart. Her experiences frustrate her and cause tremendous inner turmoil.

In fact, Rosemary's problem goes far deeper than the issue of societal limitations. It is rooted in her attitude toward intimate relationships and her low self-esteem. This has much to do with her upbringing. Her mother left the family when Rosemary was five. Her father remarried twice and she was never welcomed by her stepmothers. Rosemary grew up feeling rejected and lacking emotional nourishment.

Individuals who bear the deep scars of rejection often doubt their self-worth and question the genuineness of others' acceptance. They actually become suspicious of any friendly gesture. If someone shows interest in making friends with them they may react with hostility or skepticism. Eventually they force others into rejecting them.

This syndrome was summed up neatly by Groucho Marx, who wisecracked: "I don't want to belong to any club that will accept me as a member." In other words, people with low opinions of themselves think the only reason others actually accept them is because they don't really know what they are getting into. And yet, people with emotionally deprived upbringings crave love and acceptance. Sometimes they let themselves get into bad or exploitative situations just to win approval.

Such destructive patterns of driving others away and/or falling into harmful relationships actually reinforce the sense of rejection and worthlessness. It becomes a vicious cycle.

People growing up with a feeling of rejection can be haunted for life and totally lose objectivity in viewing themselves. All they feel is self-criticism, self-rejection and self-depreciation. Often the problem is so deep-seated that individuals are unable to recognize what is leading them into such destructive behavior.

A person like Rosemary may end up concluding that she doesn't fit in anywhere. Feeling a misfit led her into leaving the United States in the first place, in the belief that she needed a fresh start. But each place she goes, the pattern of desperation and rejection repeats itself. Again feeling the misfit, she moves on to the next place. Expatriate communities around the world are dotted with lonely self-imposed exiles like Rosemary.

To conquer this problem, the drifter has to finally stop looking for love and acceptance in a place and find it within her or himself. The first step is to recognize your own patterns. If you find yourself repeatedly falling back into the same mistakes or the same types of unhealthy relationships you should flash the red signal. Stop and think, before moving on. The desperate search for love and approval often drives people into vulnerable and unhealthy relationships. In the end, they find no relationship and no one place can really fulfill their needs. Therefore, instead of searching from outside it is necessary to find acceptance from within. Love yourself as you might love a child who has been badly hurt. Provide tenderness and care rather than criticism. Find reasons for encouragement rather than condemnation. Above all, be patient. Self-respect needs time to build.

Lastly, it would be helpful for you to understand your upbringing and relationship to your family. For example, why mother or father weren't able to provide love and care. Were they incapable of love, or were they just restricted by circumstances? Understanding that can help you to break free from the bondage of anger or resentment and learn how to deal with it rather than push it aside.

Growing up feeling rejected is one of the most painful experiences anyone can ever have. However, if people allow themselves to grasp hold of this feeling and stop it from eating them up inside, they will be spared from life-long torment. The healing process can be long and exhausting but it is also rewarding.

LONELY WORKING WOMEN—SINGLE

This is not to say that all single expatriates, male or female, are drifters or lack self-respect. But many single expatriates, women in particular, do find loneliness to be something harder to avoid and harder to deal with while living overseas.

"The thought of remaining single for the rest of my life scares the wits out of me!" Lynn, an advertising executive, has been in Asia for six years. Professionally she has reached the point where she is content and comfortable. Yet personally she feels unfulfilled.

"There seems to be absolutely no chance for me to have a love life here."

Lynn has started to question whether staying in Asia is causing her to let her career take precedent over her emotional needs.

"Back home I would have a much easier time," she explained.

During home leaves or business trips Lynn often meets interesting men and has romantic flings. Yet because of time constraints and geography, no real long-term relationship is possible.

Most people in Lynn's situation yearn for a long-term committed relationship. She dreams of having a family and children. Meanwhile, she settles for short-term affairs. As far as she is concerned, at least these affairs give her a small dose of the intimacy which is missing from her life.

She questions whether this is all she can hope for. Thus she has even begun thinking about abandoning Asia. But should individuals like Lynn return to where they came from, and would it make any difference?

There is some truth to the belief that in Asia the chances for a non-Asian female to find a partner are not as high as back in their home territory. Yet before entirely blaming the environment for the lack of opportunities, one should look at other factors.

Female professionals have to live up to a certain expected or self-imposed image in the business world. Even during social occasions both women and men find it difficult to "let their hair down": always worried about their reputations, constantly on the alert for prospective clients and business contacts. Thus someone like Lynn feels the need to maintain her cool, assertive, strong businesswoman image at all times. Men may then treat her more as a colleague or buddy than as a potential romantic partner.

When traveling Lynn is able to lower her guard more easily. She can interact with men much more freely, which enables romance to blossom more easily.

Clearly, the first step for Lynn to help herself is to compare how she interacts with men while traveling to how she interacts with them in her everyday environment. She has to remind herself to stop always being the high-powered businesswoman and let others get to know her as a person. She may feel uneasy to begin with, but unless she is willing to take some risks she will be stuck where she is.

Another notion a woman such as Lynn must resist is the fantasy that she will be rescued by a knight in shining armor. If only (she imagines to herself) on some trip abroad she meets Mr. Right, she will gladly abandon her home and her job in favor of a committed relationship. This fantasy can get out of hand. Any excuse to travel—and thus increase the chances of meeting Mr. Right—such as business, weddings, even a birthday party on the other side of the world, is latched on to. This further contributes to the confusion about where she belongs and what she is looking for.

There are many expatriate women like Lynn. Each must make an important decision: either to move to a place with a more conducive social environment and possibly accept a lesser job in that place, or to stay and work on the solution from within. Clearly the latter makes more sense. Asia may be a romantic desert for many non-Asian women, but even in the desert flowers bloom.

She should set aside a period of six months during which she will not entertain the idea of leaving, and will travel only when unavoidably necessary. By limiting her own horizons, this will force her to concentrate more fully on getting the most of what is around her. It also increases her chances of bumping into Mr. Right, right here where she lives, works and, for the time being, calls home.

LONELY WORKING WOMEN—MARRIED

"I'm so frustrated! I feel such a misfit here," said Christina, in tears. "At work I'm the boss, yet in social settings I'm the oddball."

Christina, an architect in her early forties, moved to Malaysia over twelve months ago. Both she and her husband went abroad for job advancement and are satisfied career-wise. Christina spent the past several months adjusting to the new environment and job, and now is trying to build a friendship network. To her disappointment, she finds she can't relate to most women she runs into socially.

Regardless of feminist attitudes in most Western societies, the fact of the matter is that among expatriate communities, most men work and most of their wives don't. Often this is due to language or visa restrictions. Nevertheless, it can make those women who do pursue a career abroad feel out of place.

Back home, Christina had good social support and many working female friends with whom she could share intellectually and talk about work as well as personal interests. In Kuala Lumpur she finds she has to go against great odds to make friends. When she hits it off with someone, the person may suggest. "Let's get together for afternoon tea."

"Afternoon tea! What they mean is expat women in this town don't work, and they assume you're the same," Christina said with a smirk.

111

She finds it difficult to identify with people she meets socially. "How long can a person carry on talking about antiques, jewelry or shopping?" Christina said. She finds it uncomfortable to share things she is interested in talking about, especially things related to work. She is afraid of being perceived as a show-off. She also senses other women's uneasiness around her because of their lack of common interests. She feels lonely and dissatisfied and frequently cries in front of her husband.

Christina is experiencing identity confusion. She feels distressed at not being able to identify with those who are supposed to be her peers. Though such people are of the same socio-economic level, same gender, and same or similar culture, they seem to be worlds apart from her.

She used to associate with working female professionals back home, whereas presently all she runs into are mostly non-working wives. This poses a big conflict in her. She begins to see herself more as the "weird" one than the norm, as she used to be back in her home country.

On the other hand, Christina feels somewhat righteous being part of the workforce and tends to hold herself above the other wives, who she sees as nonproductive. At the same time, she cannot help feeling jealous toward these people. They can afford not to work and enjoy having time to do things that Christina never has the leisure to do.

The ambivalence of both disapproving of and envying others' lifestyle causes her confusion. But her strong self-image as a productive working woman makes her reject the other women's way of life. Gradually she develops a self-centered attitude, colored with cynicism. Such an attitude helps turn people off, which in turn makes her more bitter. This becomes a downward spiral.

Meanwhile, her attempts to penetrate into the local community have created another disappointment. Christina finds her local Asian colleagues keep her at a distance. They may be friendly, but no one allows her to get to know them closely. In their eyes, she remains the outsider, even though they all work together.

This causes her further frustration and confusion. She doesn't seem to fit into either group. People in Christina's situation are bound to feel left out, alone and unhappy. It is not uncommon that they may question who they are.

In fact, what Christina is experiencing can be likened to culture shock. After all, she is no longer living at home and what she now encounters—the "antique and boutique clique"—is just part of the local expatriate culture. As with other local customs, one doesn't have to like or become part of it, but accept it for what it is. She needs to adapt and make the best of the situation rather than totally reject whatever is different from her former experience. Christina's need to feel useful and capable is important to her. By no means should she stop pursuing her career. However, she needs to be aware of her own cynicism. It causes her to pass hasty judgment on any foreign woman she comes across. This will further sabotage her opportunities to meet potential friends. Such an attitude also keeps her isolated and helps sustain her loneliness.

People like Christina have to learn to accept the fact that the price for their career advancement may mean some social sacrifices, particularly within the limited environment of an expatriate community. They may not be able to associate with the type of people they were used to back home. Instead of turning sour, they need to learn how to live with it and be open for new opportunities to make friends.

LONELY WORKING MEN

"Business, no problem! But when it comes to making friends I feel like a loser," Andrew said.

Andrew, a businessman in his mid-thirties, has lived in Korea for three years. He enjoys prosperity in business, but socially he is dissatisfied. He feels lonely, frustrated and without friends he can relate to.

Devoted to his business, Andrew's life very much revolves around it. He realizes that parties and social obligations are part of his job, and at these he can function well. He appears confident and comfortable in such settings.

He learned quickly that most people relate to each other in their particular defined roles of banker, diplomat, advertising executive, or whatever. Everyone talks about business or politics, or makes small talk, but rarely expresses anything even remotely personal. Andrew also slips into his own role as "successful businessman", which he finds convenient and safe. But he doesn't realize it has become a stumbling block in his attempts to make real contact with people.

He is so used to hiding behind his mask as a business person that he finds it difficult to relate to others even in informal settings. The club, parties, pub and gym are often places he makes business contacts. He tells himself, "You never know if one of these people may be a future client. It would hurt my business image if I become too personal with them." Therefore, even when meeting acquaintances and socializing, he remains superficial, detached and impersonal. On the other hand, he complains that "sometimes I want to let my hair down, but I just don't know how." Deep inside he feels lonely, left out and stuck in a twilight zone.

Andrew's problem is not exclusive to him. Many lonely people out there also put on masks. Andrew's mask is that of "self-assured, successful businessman". They can appear confident and sociable at parties and yet inside yearn for real friendships, just like Andrew.

As many people recognize, expatriate society in most countries revolves around cliques. People usually associate with others of similar social standing and/or profession. They are drawn together in business as well as in social gatherings. It is not easy to move outside one's clique, and within the group it is nearly impossible to suddenly change habitual ways of relating to each other. The common belief that "no one has time for or interest in personal issues" reinforces the continuance of relationships at a superficial level.

Andrew blames his business for causing him to be stuck in such a position. However, blame doesn't accomplish anything. Andrew must realize that he deliberately allows others only to see a certain part of himself which he feels comfortable to reveal. By doing so, he prevents people from really knowing him.

Many people like Andrew do not know how to draw a line between when to be themselves and when to don the mask. Whenever in doubt, on goes the mask and out goes any chance of getting to know others on a deeper personal level.

In order to generate real friendships you need to allow yourself to take risks, just like in business. You need to evaluate the circumstances and, if the situation permits, be more open about personal thoughts and feelings.

Drawing a clear line between work and social settings is essential. You can list the social occasions you have recently attended and determine at which of these you could have been less formal and taken off your mask. Then, when similar situations come up in the future, you can make a conscious decision as to whether to play your usual role or to be yourself. Furthermore, you can create opportunities by meeting people on a one-to-one basis, where you put away business and share personal interests.

REMOVE THOSE MASKS!

Within the small expatriate community people tend to worry that word will get around if they let down their guard. Such an attitude only encourages people to put on masks. Whether you are a Lonely Housewife or Single Woman, a Drifter, a Lonely Working Woman or Man, the problem is usually one and the same.

You have to recognize there could be others out there just like you, needing friends. You must allow yourself to reach out and openly express your difficulties in finding friends. By doing so, you will inspire others who hide behind masks to come forward and acknowledge their needs as well. Until people can express and admit the problem, they will continue to hide behind masks and remain lonely and frustrated.

Chapter 6

Daily life dilemmas

A LIFE LIKE ANY OTHER

To ANYONE WHO has lived in a foreign country beyond a year, daily life is just that: everyday life. Certainly most expatriates live privileged lives compared with the surrounding population, or compared to how they themselves lived back in their home country. But once the novelty wears off, once the culture shock is history, most of us settle into our own routines, each with our daily little triumphs and disappointments.

A lot of the problems faced by expatriates are not much different than those faced by people anywhere: marital spats, parent-teenager troubles, low self-esteem and so on. As discussed in previous chapters, many problems people face are aggravated by the expatriate lifestyle. Some, such as culture shock, are experienced only by people living abroad.

There are some common problems neither made especially worse by the expatriate lifestyle nor exclusive to it, but which are so prevalent among expatriate communities, experienced by so many people who live overseas, that they are worthy of mention.

In this chapter we will look at some of these.

WHEN PARTY TIME IS A NIGHTMARE

Entertaining and social functions make up a major portion of many expatriates' social calendars. Whether out of business or social obligation, when it's your family's turn to host a gathering, the job of organizing usually falls upon the woman of the house.

Within the small, self-contained expatriate community, the reputation stakes are high and the pressures enormous. But for anyone not used to this sort of responsibility, the results can be devastating.

> *"It was the least thing I could do for my husband, but I couldn't even do it right."*
>
> *Sue cries uncontrollably. She is in a tense and extremely anxious mood. She complains of insomnia, depression and thinking obsessively of the party she and her husband hosted a week ago.*

Back in California David was a middle-ranking executive with his bank. Sue and he lived in a comfortable home in the suburbs, but by no means had an ostentatious lifestyle. Eight months ago, David was transferred to an Asian capital to become the head of the local branch office. Suddenly, Sue and David found themselves in the elite class, living in an exclusive neighborhood with servants and limousine. Soon David found that business entertaining and social functions were part of his job. Being the banker's wife, Sue naturally assumed the role of hostess.

Although Sue had some experience in entertaining guests back home, most occasions were informal or backyard affairs. In this new upper class environment, Sue has become quite cautious and even a bit anxious whenever she needs to prepare a party. Being a quiet person by nature, she finds herself needing mental preparation before every occasion. But the recent annual party for her husband's company was almost too much for her to handle.

Her attempt to lose a few pounds before the party forced her into a battle between her diet and her agitated mood. She began to worry about not being able to fit into her new dress, tailored for the party. She also questioned whether her present hairstyle would fit the special occasion. Gradually, Sue became preoccupied with her physical appearance and mannerisms. She was overwhelmed with the thought that she would expose her ineptitude at social small-talk and be unable to impress the guests. For a whole week before the party she suffered from insomnia, which left her in an even more disheveled and anxious state.

At the party, fatigued and anxious, Sue constantly contrasted her own appearance and behavior with the wives of her husband's associates. She saw them as confident, experienced and sophisticated. But she felt herself fat, unattractive and unable to hold an intelligent conversation. She was feeling awkward and tongue-tied and finally couldn't stand facing the guests. She shut herself in the bathroom, crying. She chastised herself as a failure for not being able to fulfill her expected role.

One week after the party Sue feels even more depressed and inadequate. Though many guests sent their thanks and compliments, her own husband neglected to praise her efforts. Though she knows she shouldn't, she takes this as disapproval. She has become withdrawn and refuses to discuss her problem with David despite his show of concern.

Sue is suffering a major depressive episode. High expectations of herself and her wanting to do it right had put her in a very stressful state. Yet she chose not to turn to David for support, for worry of burdening him with "her" job.

Meanwhile, she felt herself quite alone. She was afraid to expose her weakness to her acquaintances because she feared word would get around in her small circle. Anxiety overwhelmed her, with consequent neurotic behavior. Her distress made her even less prepared to cope with the burdens of the party arrangements. The more she demanded herself to perform, the less capable she found herself. It turned into a vicious cycle. Sue concluded her performance at the party proved her to be a total failure and a worthless person.

People like Sue suffering a major depressive episode tend to view things in a negative light. They reproach themselves for minor failings and search the environment for cues confirming their negative self-evaluation. Loss of energy, insomnia, poor appetite, diminished ability to think or concentrate and feelings of worthlessness are common symptoms.

In order to deal with such a situation one needs to gain a better understanding of how mainly trivial incidents can lead to such distress. Someone in Sue's situation needs to be more sensitive to herself and her own patterns of stress accumulation. She should learn to recognize the physical signs or symptoms and realize that her worries and over-anxiety could be signs of stress.

Sue should simply talk about the fears with her husband and close friends prior to the party. Removing the air of secrecy will release much of the anxiety. It will then be less difficult to admit inexperience in hosting a party and to ask for help.

The most practical way to deal with a stressful situation like this is to get organized. List things that need to be done for the party ahead of time and set priorities to tackle them one by one. If anxiety arises during the preparations, slow down and do some relaxation exercises. The hostess needs to constantly remind herself not to push past her own limits. With self-awareness, organization and outside support, a hostess can handle her duty without putting herself through unnecessary anguish.

VISITORS ARE STRESSFUL!

Most people living far away from their home country or region will eventually receive visitors, often with an expectation, spoken or unspoken, of accommodation. As enjoyable as it is to be together again with family or friends, if the visit is over an extended period of time, it can be stressful.

Ann's parents are visiting from Toronto for six weeks. The first two weeks were fine but as the days go by, both Ann and her husband are feeling overwhelmed and stressful.

"Besides taking care of my son, suddenly I feel like I have two other kids on my hands," Ann said.

Being visited by parents, other family members or friends is a joyful experience. However, the preparations prior to the visit can be quite exhausting. Organizing the house, shopping for extra food, making arrangements for guests' entertainment and trying to clear your work schedule are no easy tasks.

When the guest finally arrives the host needs to make him or herself continually available for advice on getting around, where to shop without being ripped off, how to behave in the foreign culture, and making sure the guests are having a good time. All these are real work.

Sightseeing, too, may lose its sparkle when it's the eighth time in three months you have taken visitors around to all the major local tourist attractions. You may not care to ever take another glance at the spectacular view from an overpriced revolving restaurant or jostle the crowds at must-see landmarks that you've seen a thousand times. Yet the honored guests would be disappointed to have to go on their own. It can become an annoyance rather than pleasure.

If the guests are parents then obviously more responsibilities are assumed. In a foreign land, visiting parents will depend on their children—not only as hosts, but as ambassadors or cultural go-betweens. There, far away from the old family home, the children are the masters of the household and the parents the dependents, being guided and taught how to behave and not behave in the foreign country. In a way the child takes up the role of parent.

Role reversal creates confusion for both child and parents. Frequent reminders by the children about where to go or how to act, or constant questions and requests from the parents, can cause both sides annoyance, which is easily misinterpreted as disrespect or lack of appreciation. Sometimes a parent's cultural *faux pas* can cause embarrassment. If this goes on without clarification it can lead to hurt feelings between parents and child.

Such tensions should not reach serious proportions during a short visit. But when retired parents choose to visit for an extended stay it can upset the whole family balance. The couple and their immediate family may begin to get irritated and long for more space and privacy.

People in Ann's situation will experience various kinds of stress. Trying to fulfill all her roles as mother, wife, daughter, hostess and care-provider at the same time may cause her to become exasperated. Yet having such negative feelings is also guilt-provoking and could be taken as a sign of rejecting her parents. Therefore these feelings are often denied, which itself can turn into a further source of stress.

It is important for the host and hostess to remind themselves of their own limitations in terms of energy, space, time and tolerance for lack of privacy. In order to maximize the pleasure and minimize the stress and inconvenience, it would be helpful to discuss the plan with the guests long before they arrive. Just because they want to stay two weeks does not oblige you to agree. Clarify far in advance how long they will be welcome to stay and how much time the host can spend with them.

It is essential to set a realistic schedule for spending time with visitors. One mistake many hosts or hostesses commit is over-extending themselves, as well as overwhelming their guests by trying to do too much in too little time. Learn to give the responsibility back to the guests of determining what they want to do during their visit. Let them do their own exploring. This probably will give them a more fun experience.

As far as reversed roles is concerned, the child has to recognize and remind him or herself that this is only temporary. Instead of resenting it he or she should allot time for privacy and personal pursuits.

When necessary, say "no" to guests. Often visitors assume that since they are on holiday the host or hostess is also free to take time off. Thus it is up to the host or hostess to be honest with their visitors. If both sides respect each other's priorities, they will better share the pleasurable moments together, which may not happen often.

Expatriate addictions

Just as seemingly trivial problems, such as parties and visitors, can escalate into personal crises, so too apparently harmless activities can develop into harmful, self-destructive behavior. Most addictions start this way.

Addictions, though, are not usually a matter of a personal habit getting out of hand. Usually they are rooted in deeper psychological problems. The same problem can manifest itself in different addictions, whether to alcohol, tranquilizers or compulsive gambling. Any addictive behavior must be taken seriously and treated before it destroys a person's family or life.

Expatriates are no more and no less prone to addictive syndromes than the population as a whole. However, aside from the leading addictions—tobacco and alcohol—there are two types of addiction very commonly found among expatriates, both related to consumption: compulsive eating and compulsive spending.

COMPULSIVE EATING

Louise, 28, has been fighting a weight problem for over three years, ever since her youngest son was born.

"I've tried every diet possible, but it only works for a while, then I put back on again," Louise claims.

Louise feels her weight problem was triggered by hormonal changes during her second pregnancy. She tried for a long time to reduce her weight, but after three years she still finds herself caught between binging and dieting.

Her husband George has become critical of her appearance and occasionally makes derogatory remarks about her in front of friends. She complains that her husband doesn't have time for her and she finds it difficult to talk to him about her frustration.

She expressed mild regret for having the second child.

Louise is unhappy with herself and feels the weight problem is affecting her self-image and self-confidence. She believes once she can tackle her weight problem she will be much happier.

Superficially, her weight seems to be the cause of her problems and dissatisfaction. Yet upon further exploration, it is clear that her weight problem is only the symptom of a deeper issue which had not been recognized.

Louise's weight problem is not necessarily caused by only one factor. It could be a combination of hormonal changes, poor diet, poor impulse control and problems in family life.

According to Louise, she was pregnant with her second child four months after relocating overseas. Soon after that her husband was promoted to Regional Director of his company. The new position required that George travel more frequently. With the arrival of the new family member and her husband frequently away from home, the family was forced to restructure on two levels at once.

Within a family, each member has a role which he or she is comfortable with. Family members will unconsciously shift roles to adapt to changes in the family situation. Louise's family has adapted to a new triangular arrangement of mother and two children.

Since the family is running smoothly without George's frequent presence, gradually they have become comfortable with the new family structure.

Changes in family structure are subtle and hard to recognize. When the change is caused by a seemingly positive event—George's promotion—it is that much more difficult to acknowledge.

Louise has very much become both mother and father to the two children. From household decisions to child discipline, everything falls on her shoulders. Even when George is home Louise remains in command. To some extent, George's contribution, other than financial, has become limited and less significant.

In practical terms, Louise has no trouble meeting the needs of the family. However, when it comes to her own need for spousal companionship and support, and for emotional and physical affection, she is in a state of desperation. During her limited time alone with her husband she tries not to overwhelm him with her troubles. Instead of spilling out her feelings she forces them back. Emotionally, she has an empty hole inside her, needing to be filled.

Eating is her way of filling the hole. The lonelier she feels, the more she eats. The more she feels cut off emotionally, the more frequently she tends to nibble. When she isn't pleased with how she looks and feels, she becomes depressed and dissatisfied. Momentary relief comes by indulging in food. Such a pattern becomes a vicious cycle.

Tackling an eating problem requires dealing with the habitual eating and the underlying causes simultaneously. Reining in the habit of overeating is only half of the process. One needs to set reachable goals to reduce eating between meals and follow an appropriate diet. Overeaters Anonymous is a good source of support in dealing with habitual eating.

At the same time, it is important to gain an understanding of the causes, beginning with analysis of the eating patterns.

WHAT CIRCUMSTANCES TRIGGER A BINGE?

Most people binge when they are frustrated, lonely, or want to shut off their minds and seek temporary gratification.

WHAT IS IT YOU REALLY WANT AT THAT PARTICULAR MOMENT, OTHER THAN FOOD?

Do you want companionship? Or do you want privacy? Is there a project or activity you'd rather be working on right now? Or would you rather be relaxing by the pool or with friends in a café? Once people pay attention to their own behaviors, thoughts and feelings, they will be able to become aware of their own needs and really deal with the root of the problem rather than using food as a temporary relief. Most people with an eating problem will not talk about it with family or friends. Therefore professional help is often necessary. Compulsive eating will not only destroy a person's self-esteem, but also his or her physical health. If the problem continues, it can lead to other self-destructive behavior, such as substance abuse. Unless appropriate treatment is taken, a person will never be free from daily, self-imposed torment.

COMPULSIVE SPENDING

"I often buy outfits I never end up wearing," Cindy said. "I know I shouldn't have bought them, but shopping always cheers me up. It makes me feel alive."

Cindy, 34, moved to Taiwan sixteen months ago. Her husband has gotten on her case lately over her spending habits. She feels ashamed and depressed.

"In fact, he's right about me. It doesn't matter how much he gives me, I end up spending it all. I'm really no good with money."

Cindy is a compulsive spender. Although she recognizes that she exceeds the family budget, she can't resist her impulses. She ends up feeling guilty and frustrated for over-extending herself financially, but the more frustrated she feels, the more she spends.

Compulsive spending may not sound like a serious problem to most people, but in fact it is a form of addiction. It is no different from other material addictions, such as pathological gambling or kleptomania.

Not all enthusiastic shoppers are problem spenders. The signals that a problem exists are when you feel little or no control over your impulses, or you repeatedly buy things that are never used.

Compulsive spending is caused by both social and psychological factors. Expatriates in particular are vulnerable to this specific problem. It affects equally both men and women, but is often more visible among female expatriates.

Many working wives accompanying their husbands overseas must either totally give up their careers or settle for something other than their chosen profession because of limited opportunities. Others find their former role as homemaker taken over by their live-in maid. Feeling lonely and frustrated, they often use shopping and dining out as a way of feeling better about themselves.

The modern urban lifestyle, with its emphasis on consumption and acquisition, certainly promotes the impulse to spend. All the latest fashions and electronic gadgets besiege our vision at every turn in almost every major city on earth. Elsewhere, ethnic handicrafts, jewelry, antiques and artifacts inspire the "collector" in us. Fancy boutiques and pricey cafés provide limitless opportunities for people to consume and spend beyond their limit. Such temptations often are difficult to resist. Peer pressure to possess luxury brands too often makes it feel mandatory.

The nouveau riche syndrome also encourages spending. Many middle class families arrive in a foreign posting and suddenly find themselves among the elite of society. New-found affluence and the need to keep up appearances encourage them to upgrade their lifestyle accordingly.

However, affluence and temptation alone do not cause compulsive spending. The key problem is a psychological one. The act of spending is stimulating, providing immediate gratification. For example, buying a new dress makes someone feel good about herself. At that particular moment there is an uplift of self-image and boost of self-confidence. There is a surge of adrenaline which can become psychologically as well as physically addicting, as with any stimulant.

During the course of spending, the overspender may experience a sense of pleasure, gratification or release. But often following the act he or she will feel regret, self-reproach or guilt. The feeling is relieved only by another shopping binge. This turns into a cycle that is difficult to get out of.

People suffering from emotional turmoil or poor self-esteem are vulnerable to this sort of addiction. They use shopping as a way to temporarily lift them from depression or fill a void in their life. In Cindy's case, when she feels depressed she tends to spend more. It helps her "feel more alive."

Compulsive spenders often spend money in order to gain approval and acceptance from others, by treating friends to fancy dinners, buying presents, and so on. Though their budget may be stretched to the limit, the reward of being accepted and appreciated is far more important than the money spent.

Though this problem is mostly identified with women, expatriate men, too, are vulnerable to spending addiction, though often for slightly different reasons. They may accumulate expensive hardware, such as cars, mobile phones, new watches, home entertainment and sports equipment, as well as designer clothes. Probing deeper, though, we are likely to find a person attempting to compensate for his own perceived inadequacies.

The way to deal with compulsive spending is first to focus on the spending behavior itself. Consciously avoid opportunities to consume and keep away from areas full of buying temptations. Restricting your access to money by canceling credit and automatic teller cards can help discourage impulsive spending.

It is important to realize, however, that compulsive spending is caused by feelings of unfulfillment, insecurity, and self-deprecation. The battle is against low self-esteem rather than a financial budget. Thus, dealing with compulsive spending requires more than merely cutting up the credit cards or avoiding high-priced boutiques.

You must look deeper within yourself to understand why there is such a need and what triggers it. Making positive efforts toward finding a genuine source of fulfillment in life is the surest cure for self-destructive—and expensive—behavior.

FEAR OF FLYING

As with addictions, phobias are commonplace among the general population. Almost everyone has some sort of phobia at one time or another. Most have little or no affect on people's lives, but some phobias can genuinely interfere.

Perhaps half the people from developed countries have a fear of flying. For one in ten, the fear is so intense that it can be considered a phobia. This proportion is probably smaller among expatriate communities, simply because people with a pronounced fear of flying would be less inclined take a job that required them to frequently travel by air. Nowadays, most expatriate executives find themselves in an airplane anywhere from several times a year to several times a week.

There are reasons to dread flying. No means of mechanical transport is absolutely safe, and on a case-by-case basis air accidents, more often than auto or train crashes, involve fatalities. However, statistically air travel has far fewer fatalities per distance traveled than any other means of transport, and most people still favor air travel for its speed and convenience, benefits which outweigh the miniscule risks. Nevertheless, even frequent flyers can develop a fear of flying. For an expatriate whose job requires regular air travel, this little phobia can turn him into a nervous wreck.

"It's just like the worst nightmare. I dread to even think of flying. It seems to be getting worse and worse."

James, 36, is a hotel executive. One of his major responsibilities is to oversee and supervise his regional managers. Traveling has always been part of his job. About eight months ago he began to develop a fear of flying. Every time he travels he becomes preoccupied with worries about turbulence, plane crashes or hijacks. He now dreads business trips and canceled all unnecessary travel, including his family's summer holiday, in order to avoid flying.

In general, James feels content and in control of his life. However, his fear of flying frustrates him. He begins to question what's wrong with him. "One of these days I'll lose my job because of this," he said.

James's fear of flying has become a phobia.

A phobia is a persistent and irrational fear of a specific object, activity or situation. For example, reading the news about a plane crash or emergency causes James to develop intense anxiety. As he waits at the airport, he breaks into a sweat. He anticipates being the next victim of an air disaster. The idea of getting on an airplane is almost unbearable. Once on board, his body goes stiff and he is unable to relax. He drinks excessively to calm himself. His mind and body together are reacting to fear.

Flying can be both physiologically and psychologically stressful. The long hours sitting in one position are tiring. It also disrupts the biological rhythms of sleep and digestion. Low humidity as a result of cabin pressurization at high altitude dehydrates a person, which can cause discomfort and light-headedness. Dehydration and its resultant effects are heightened by drinking alcohol. Even carbonated drinks served on board can contribute to the general feeling of disorientation, as they reduce the amount of oxygen in the blood.

The low stimulation and restricted activities on a long flight give people time to focus more on the flying. A person who already perceives flying as dangerous will constantly scan the environment for signs of impending disaster: weather conditions, wing movements, checking emergency exits, and so on. Such worrying overrides most attempts at detached, rational thinking.

Feelings of confinement, helplessness, and being out of control are often present behind flying phobia. Intellectually, people know they aren't really risking their life when taking a flight. That's why they allow themselves to board the plane in the first place. However, rational and intellectual thinking often aren't able to ease irrational anxieties. The fact is, once a person is on the plane he doesn't have control of the vehicle. He is at the mercy of the pilot, powerless, with no means of escape.

Undeniably, many people will have some concern about not being in control, but some take it to extremes. They become overwhelmed by their own imaginations and magnify the real dangers of the flight. They are no longer in command of their thoughts but are seized by negative automatic thinking and anxiety. They begin to imagine the most terrible tragedies and dangerous scenarios that could possibly happen to them. The slightest bump of turbulence prompts visions of falling out of the sky. One fear builds on another. Such thinking can have a snowball effect, which will devastate a person and make him or her unable to cope.

In order to overcome fear of flying it is important to become aware of your patterns of negative thinking. When negative thoughts invade your mind, applying the "thought-stopping technique" can be helpful. Simply say "stop" under your breath to interrupt the flow of morbid thoughts. Then put a positive, rational thought in its place. For example, when turbulence makes you tense up, remind yourself that no airliner has ever crashed solely because of bumpy air. Obtaining more knowledge about how an airplane operates can also help eliminate unnecessary fear.

In addition, avoid alcohol, soft drinks and salty snacks, since these will further dehydrate your body and reduce oxygen in the bloodstream, making you more delirious. Sitting back and breathing slowly will enable the mind to be in control.

Like most phobias, fear of flying takes time to overcome. This specific phobia has been the focus of many studies, and a number of techniques for treating it have been tried and tested over the years. Most methods involve a form of systematic desensitization. This is a step-by-step method of eliminating a phobia or fear through structured exercises. A person learns how to relax while imagining scenes related to flying that are progressively more anxiety-provoking. Different types of anxiety management, such as breathing exercises, bodily relaxation and cognitive restructuring can be helpful.

Fear of flying is not easy to overcome on one's own. There are numerous specialized books and self-hypnosis programs which provide detailed and useful techniques for people who experience flying phobia: a small investment which will greatly improve the quality of a frequent traveler's life.

Chapter 7

Coping with separation

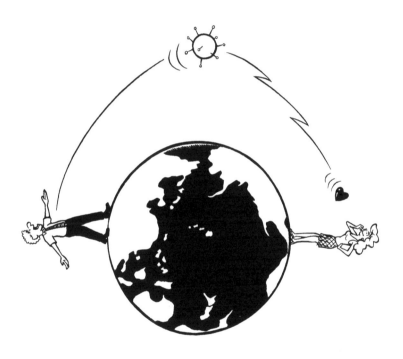

PEOPLE PULLED APART

FAREWELL PARTIES ARE a regular part of the expatriate social calendar. Whether or not you plan to relocate within the next year, chances are that someone you know will. Like it or not, separation is an unavoidable fact of life for all who live overseas.

Leaving behind colleagues and friends is something which, while painful, most expatriates must get used to. It's the flip side to the constant influx of new acquaintances into the ever-changing foreign social circle. However, it is different when the person you're saying goodbye to is a lover or spouse.

In Chapter One ("Transient Family Syndrome") we saw how a life on the move can draw people closer together, maybe even too close. In this chapter, we will look at what happens when circumstances pull people apart.

LONG-DISTANCE LOVE

One of the most painful aspects of working abroad is leaving behind loved ones back home or being separated from a newly-found loved one because of a transfer of assignment. Naturally, couples stay in touch electronically and by telephone. Each will feel a rush of excitement at every message or phone call. At the first opportunity, a holiday or business trip becomes a chance to see each other again.

Yet many people in this situation will return from a holiday reunion feeling awkward and unsure. This can be demoralizing and depressing. But if long-distance couples know what to expect, and are honest and realistic, a relationship can survive the separation of both time and distance.

"We're now engaged, and yet I feel I don't really know him anymore." May finishes with a sigh.

May and John are in their late twenties, both expatriates with promising careers. They met while both were posted in Tokyo and fell passionately in love. Eight months later, John was transferred back to Canada. During the following nine months they were in close contact through e-mails, texting, voice and video calls, and even old-fashioned love letters. Eventually May took two weeks off to visit her sweetheart.

May returned from the visit feeling unsure about the relationship and therefore sought counseling.

"We didn't fight or anything and yet I feel depressed. Something seems missing inside me." May complained that John "wasn't as sensitive, loving and witty" as he presented himself in his communications and she wonders what went wrong with their relationship.

May is disappointed that John seems to be different from what she thought he was. In a long-distance relationship, it is not easy for a person to have an objective view of the other. Without the presence of the other person, we can only grasp hold of an image in our memories. People have a natural tendency to remember only the good times and the best qualities of a loved one, which makes us miss that person even more. Differences and arguments are long forgotten.

In addition, the affectionate notes and sweet phone conversations reconfirm the "perfect" image of the absentee. We reinforce this by fantasizing or projecting an idealized image onto the person without even realizing it. Inevitably, some unreal assumptions about each other take hold. When this carries on long enough without clarification, it is no wonder two people will think each other different from several months before.

For May and John, the long distance restricts them from being in touch with each other's personal growth. Written and voice communication are more direct than ever nowadays, yet such exchanges still place a filter over expressions of thoughts and feelings. The distance and lack of personal contact can inspire a certain sense of hyperbole and drama onto the situation. Offhand little text messages may have different connotations from thousands of kilometers away than when they will be seeing each other that evening. There is a sense that certain issues can be postponed until they meet again. Over time, discussions can begin to take on an unreal quality that may not be present when the couple is together.

The long separation, loneliness, and longing for John's company brought out a lot of expectations for the two-week visit, in which everything was to be wonderful.

Couples in John and May's situation naturally feel pressured by the brevity of their visits together. The excitement of seeing each other again and their wanting to give each other a good impression can easily make them unconsciously avoid airing their differences, let alone voicing any critical comments or disagreement. They may purposely avoid conflicts or arguments in order not to spoil the brief happy time together.

In fact, this is a crucial time to catch up with each other, for direct and honest dialogue which will help them to gain a better understanding of each other's changed values and expectations. Further discussion of issues that they were unable to discuss face-to-face is essential.

During the visit, May realized that John was different from the image she had formulated. The contrast between the real person and the idealized image was something which May found hard to accept. She felt cheated and resentful that she had saved herself so long for this "ideal" guy.

The bitterness of investing so much of her time, energy and resources in this relationship has raised tremendous anger in her. All her dreams of having a compatible future partner have been shattered. She grieves for the loss of her idealized John. All she sees is that the person she supposedly was in love with for the last year and a half turned out to be a stranger to her.

As for the future of their relationship, instead of denying the problem or breaking up, May needs to deal with it more constructively, by openly communicating with John and honestly discussing their feelings and differences. Only then can they rationally make any future commitments.

Regardless of the obstacles in a long-distance relationship, many people still find it rewarding. It is likely to be successful if people are especially sensitive to issues of expectations and idealization. Both must be willing to accept their separate personal growth, give time to understand each other's values and thinking, and to honestly discuss both positive and negative feelings between them. Premarital counseling, from their clergy member or a qualified counselor will help the couple to objectively clarify their similarities and differences, set realistic expectations, and prepare themselves for a happy life together.

HOME ISN'T ALWAYS
WHERE THE HEART IS

What's true for long-distance lovers can also be true for absent family, friends, and even a place. We all tend to romanticize people and things we've left behind.

"Home is where the heart is" is a poetic notion. But if the heart isn't where the body is, it can make more than one person suffer.

> *"No one seems to understand what I'm going through. They only think I'm having a good time here," Shirley said.*

Shirley, a former nurse, moved to Thailand with her architect husband fourteen months ago. She tried to locate work in her profession but found it impossible because of language constraints. She pursues other interests and studies and still has plenty of free time on her hands. Bored, feeling a misfit in a foreign country, and homesick, she takes any opportunity to fly back to Australia for a visit—to see her mother, for a grandparent's birthday, girlfriend's baby shower, and so on.

Her frequent journeys home were intended to recapture the good old feelings. Yet Shirley sensed a new-found distance between herself and her friends. They repeatedly reminded her of how lucky she is. They envy the travel, the luxury of having a live-in maid and the fancy expatriate lifestyle Shirley enjoys.

Her friends having painted a rosy picture of her life in an exotic foreign land, Shirley felt almost compelled to live up to the image. When she tried to point out the disadvantages, they dismissed her "grumbling" as false humility. Quietly she swallowed the complaints and dissatisfaction. With no one to whom she can pour her heart out, her high hopes of re-experiencing the old closeness and support with friends and relatives all but disappeared.

Back in Bangkok, Shirley's husband Jeffrey has been very understanding of his wife's frustration.

Though he feels lonely during her frequent absences, nevertheless he encourages her to travel back to Australia if she believes it will help her. Jeffrey at the same time is making headway in building up his own network. His job is demanding but rewarding. Through work he is meeting lots of people and making friends. Naturally, he feels more settled in the new environment.

When people move to a foreign country it isn't surprising that some may be tempted to return home often. However, for individuals like Shirley, there are probably some real triggering issues behind her frequent flights home.

Shirley views most things in the new country as temporary. For her, home is still back in Australia and she believes making new friends is a waste of time and effort.

At the same time, she resents having let Jeffrey's career advancement dominate over hers. Because of him she gave up her job, friends and community status. Deep inside she feels she is losing control. Returning home is her way of not letting go of what she had and of not giving in to Jeffrey and the situation after all.

Shirley runs home to Australia to relieve her frustration at living in a foreign place. When she feels bad, she hops on a plane. This is like taking an aspirin for a toothache. The pain may subside, but unless the underlying problem is treated, the discomfort will always reappear.

She feels like the victim of the situation, but she is in fact unconsciously sabotaging herself from making any adjustments. Such behavior indicates unspoken aggression on her part: She refuses to give in to living in Thailand. This is probably an extension of her resentment at submitting to her husband's wish to move there in the first place.

Shirley's frequent visits home deprive her of the chance of ever feeling settled down. After all, she never sticks around long enough to build her own social support. By distancing herself from Bangkok, by not making an effort to find a niche for herself, by not allowing time for real friendships to develop, she is reinforcing her own dissatisfaction at living there. It is another vicious cycle.

As Shirley has found out, each return trip becomes less satisfying than the last. Eventually she may feel rootless both in Bangkok and Australia. Furthermore, the delay in resolving her feeling towards her husband can put a damper on their relationship, which will wreak destruction in their marriage.

She realizes that Jeffrey is committed to remaining in Thailand for the duration of his contract. She is trying, for his sake, to not interfere with his career. Running home enables Shirley to soothe her own unpleasant feelings and delay confrontation with her husband. But her resentment and hostility remain. The longer she avoids dealing with them, the more likely the problem will be diverted into other areas and become more difficult to deal with. This will most likely come out in the marital relationship itself.

Shirley has to come to terms with her life. She must face the fact that the "foreign" country is "home" for the duration of their stay. With this frame of mind, she can put more effort into settling in and building her support network, instead of constantly looking elsewhere. Fleeing home only prolongs and postpones the process.

People like Shirley need to be honest with themselves as to whether they are running home to avoid unpleasant feelings or situations. Confronting with such feelings is essential. Denying the feelings will only cause further confusion and misunderstanding. The spouse of someone like Shirley may think he is being understanding by encouraging her to run home. In fact, he is only helping her to avoid confronting the problems. He needs to encourage her to openly voice her troubles and complaints. Together they must directly evaluate the situation, without blame, and seek ways to accommodate both their needs.

It would be helpful prior to relocation for couples to openly and honestly discuss the pros and cons. After several months of settling down, do a review and evaluation of any unpleasant feelings that have built up.

RUNNING HOME TO A SICK PARENT

Running home is sometimes unavoidable, especially when someone there needs you. When a parent or loved one becomes disabled or critically ill, it is natural for a son or daughter to want to be there to help and provide comfort. But, as in the previous case, this also raises the question of where one's loyalties lie.

"I often think to myself: this may be the last time I see my mother, so I'd better go back," Diane said.

Diane, an expatriate wife in her mid-forties, has been living abroad for the last fifteen years with her husband and three children. Her 82-year-old widowed mother recently developed heart problems. Last year Diane spent two months back in England taking care of her. During the previous eight months, as her mother's condition deteriorated, she has flown back and forth between Hong Kong and England several times.

"I am absolutely exhausted. I can't tell you how guilty I feel leaving her there alone when she needs me the most," she wept. Diane has her hands full. She feels responsible for her aging mother, as well as her own family and children. She tries to be strong and take care of everybody, but deep inside she wants to run away.

Most people feel indebted to their parents. When they are confronted with the reality that their parents may die soon, many people find it hard to accept, especially if they live far away. They may blame themselves or unconsciously resent their spouse for their moving away.

For Diane, the fact that she has been living abroad, thousands of kilometers apart from her mother, rarely bothered her in the past. But now, having realized that her mother will not live forever, guilt wells up within her. The idea of abandoning her and depriving her of seeing the grandchildren grow up causes Diane many regrets.

Diane has to come to terms with her relationship with her elderly mother. During the many years abroad, she never felt an endearing closeness between them. But like many other adult children, she feels compelled to offer her love during the fading moments of her mother's life, only to find out there is a big gap between them. The emptiness soon turns into overwhelming sadness. Many ask themselves: "Why didn't I get to know him more?" or "Why did she make herself such a difficult person to like?" Feelings of guilt or resentment torment many adult caretakers.

Running back home to rescue an ailing parent is a way many people attempt to compensate for guilt and for not having spent time with them in the past.

However, in Diane's case, her frequent returns to England have a negative impact on her family in Hong Kong. The whole family, especially the children, have to struggle to cope during her absence. Her frequent travel inevitably causes tension between Diane and her husband. What's more, whenever the family has a holiday, the destination must always be England, in order to call on Diane's mother. Family members feel Diane puts her mother above everybody else. They resent her mother as an outside interference to the marriage and family life.

In fact, running back every time something is not right may not be helpful for the parent. It causes a role reversal situation: the child now becomes protector to the parent. This can reinforce a sense of helplessness in many elderly people. In fact, most are very capable and independent. Having another adult hovering over them can be as overbearing as an overprotective parent is to a child.

At the same time, adult children have to understand their own limitations and inability to cope with the stress of taking care of elderly parents. An individual like Diane puts her life on hold because she anticipates the need to run home any time. This not only disrupts family life but also causes her to feel out of control of her own life. If the situation is prolonged, people like her may resent the parent for putting them through this. Sometimes the frustration may be inflicted in turn on the elders, in the form of aggressive behavior or abuse.

Diane needs to have more realistic expectations of herself as a caretaker. Since she cannot always be physically present it is important that she arrange some help that can lessen any pain or danger to her mother; for example, a live-in nurse or assisted living center. Keeping regular contact through phone and e-mail will offer comfort and assurance that her mother is being cared for.

Diane also needs to draw a line between her mother's needs and those of her own nuclear family. She has to carry on her life, accept her own limitations and believe that she is doing her very best within the constraints of geographical distance. Finally, she needs to try not to force her mother's problems onto the whole family.

THE ASTRONAUT SYNDROME

When one partner in a marriage is truly dissatisfied with living in a foreign country, the couple may have to make the difficult choice of one of them returning home while the other finishes out an overseas contract term. In other cases, one spouse will stay behind from the beginning, usually so as not to sacrifice his or her own career. Either way, such couples are facing the "Astronaut Syndrome".

Randolf complains that all he has in China is work and more work. "I miss my wife and son terribly. I really can't see the end of this two-year separation."

Randolf, age 37, an executive with a shoe manufacturer, was sent to China for two years to oversee the setting up of a new factory near Guangzhou. This was a good opportunity for career enhancement, as well as to earn extra money. However, because his wife has her own job back home in Austria, he went to China by himself, while returning home every chance he can. He recently came back from a six-week visit with his wife and three-year-old son.

In Guangzhou he lives in a comfortable hotel apartment, and has made acquaintances among the other foreign residents. He works extra hours in order to build up longer leave time for his visits home. However, he finds it hard to accept his new "bachelor" lifestyle. All at once he finds himself having no emotional outlets.

Randolf feels lonesome, unhappy and vulnerable. He has tremendous responsibility on his shoulders, yet he finds himself depressed and unmotivated in his work.

Randolf is experiencing what most "astronauts" experience. An "astronaut" is a married person who goes abroad on a temporary assignment to earn money or for career purposes, while the spouse and children stay behind in the home country. Husband and wife communicate regularly over long distance, but both have to endure a great deal of stress. The marriage inevitably goes through a tremendous trial.

Even though he and his wife had long prepared for the separation, Randolf still isn't immune from its effects. He has no one to come home to after work. All he can think of is the good old days and how much he wishes he were in Austria with his family. Knowing he cannot watch his son grow up for two crucial years of his life makes him sad and lonely. His original plan of furthering his career for the sake of his family turns out feeling like a trap.

Most of his foreign friends in Guangzhou are either genuine bachelors or have their families with them. Thus they find it difficult to empathize with his loneliness and inner turmoil. Randolf inevitably avoids sharing his frustrations with them. Meanwhile, when speaking or writing to his wife, he keeps up a happy front, so as not to add to her own list of worries.

He buries himself in work to fill his emptiness. At the same time, he deprives himself of leisure activities, including joining friends for weekends in Hong Kong, in order to save money. He feels guilty spending anything on himself.

He took this overseas assignment in the first place in order to produce more income. He has convinced himself that the more he can save up, the more the sacrifice will have been worth it.

Depriving yourself is not the way to deal with an extended separation. After all, a person cannot stop living until reunited with the spouse. Maintaining a healthy social life is vital to an individual's mental health.

Meanwhile, it is essential that both spouses put extra effort into communicating their fears, worries, positive and negative feelings to each other. Through such emotional exchange, a couple can provide mutual support and maintain a sense of closeness. In addition, regular visits should be scheduled so that both partners have something to look forward to, making separation more tolerable.

People in such situations have difficulties not only during the extended separation, but also when they get back together. Both sides have made many sacrifices. Naturally, they have high expectations for the reunion. But the fact is, the couple haven't lived with each other for several years.

As in long-distance relationships in general, when couples separate, they tend to think of the good qualities of the other and forget the defects. When they encounter each other again later they are reminded of all the past annoyances or negative aspects of their spouse. What's more, acculturation and other factors may have made them grow apart from one another. One or both may find it difficult to accept the changes or differences between them.

At the other extreme, if the marriage was shaky to begin with, a long separation will encourage their lives to take different directions. If this is the case, there is obviously a high risk of infidelity on one side or the other. In either case, the reunion can quickly become a permanent separation or divorce unless special care is given to the marital relationship.

The "astronaut" phenomenon is becoming increasingly common among the international business community, as well as among professional classes of immigrants, including Astronaut Syndrome in reverse, prevalent among Asian families, in which the family moves abroad to claim another nationality, while the working spouse remains behind to continue his profession.

More people will face Randolf's dilemma of having to choose between family life and career opportunities. Of course, when decisions are being made, a balance should be struck between the two. More important is to take into consideration the emotional aspects, which will not only affect the marital relationship but also the whole family's welfare.

Chapter 8

Death and divorce

DIVORCE IN A FOREIGN LAND

SOMETIMES ONE PARTNER within a marriage is unhappy or unfulfilled by living overseas. Often one spouse travels frequently and has little time left over for the family. When problems like these are left unresolved, divorce can be the tragic result.

The divorce rate among expatriates is generally high. The reasons for divorce are no different than among the population as a whole. However, as pointed out elsewhere, many problems are aggravated by the expatriate lifestyle.

Divorce can be a complicated matter overseas. In some countries it is simply illegal or extremely difficult. Others require lengthy waiting periods or periods of official separation before a divorce can proceed.

Many divorces are preventable. But when the decision to divorce has been mutually agreed upon, people living overseas must deal with it emotionally as they would in any other place. Unfortunately, things can be made more difficult for divorcees within a small, gossip-ridden expatriate community.

FIVE TYPES OF DIVORCE

Divorce is a difficult and painful process for anyone to endure. It is the termination of a family unit, inevitably having a great impact on both partners and their children.

Divorcees have to come to grips with the fact that ending a marriage is much more than just "breaking up".

Every divorce is actually five separations all at once:

EMOTIONAL DIVORCE: Ripping apart what was built up emotionally over the years. Breaking off an emotional dependence can cause a person to feel extremely insecure and lonely.

LEGAL DIVORCE: A battleground which many view as the last chance to fight back and exact revenge. It is also an expensive and draining process.

ECONOMIC DIVORCE: Dividing possessions and assets, as well as altering one's lifestyle to reflect the new economic reality.

CO-PARENTAL DIVORCE: A couple will no longer be raising their children together. This means added responsibilities for the custodial parent, and the threat of alienation from the children for the non-custodial parent.

SOCIAL DIVORCE: A newly single person is forced into making changes in terms of identity, status and social groups.

BEREAVEMENT

"I'm just no longer the same person. I feel haunted by my ex-husband," June said sadly.

June, 45 years old, has been living in Singapore. She divorced about nine months ago after a seventeen-year marriage. She claimed the marriage was stable until she discovered her husband's affair. They went through a long, bitter period of fighting before they decided on divorce. June went to stay with her sister in Sydney for three months right after her divorce was final.

Being a strong-willed person, June was determined to make it on her own. She had worked for many years as a language teacher in Singapore. She wasn't about to sacrifice her position or leave the country she had made her home just because of the divorce. She returned to Singapore, moved to a new apartment and resumed practicing her profession. She felt that the three months away had helped her to forget her pain. She was surprised to find herself getting over the trauma so quickly.

However, June's lifestyle has become more sheltered. She avoids contact with places and people associated with her ex-husband. She discarded all those items that remind her of him.

Things went fine until two months ago. Through an acquaintance she heard that her former husband, also still in Singapore, would be getting remarried. Suddenly, she became hypersensitive. Inexplicable rage kept building up. She went through a stage of crying spells and found herself unable to perform her job.

June is experiencing delayed bereavement. She lost her husband and a stable married life through the divorce, yet she hasn't given herself a chance to grieve over the loss and hurt.

She had tried to deal with the reality of her divorce by distancing herself from the reminders. Her time away from Singapore, then avoiding any former contacts, and moving to a new home, all simply enabled her to evade painful memories. But when confronted by the fact of her husband's remarriage, suddenly the agony of her loss is reactivated.

Bereavement is a process that we must go through whenever we experience a loss. It provides an opportunity for us to grieve and to accept and deal with the loss. Bereavement is not only something we go through when a person has died. It is part of getting over any loss, including marriage breakup or disability. In different circumstances the loss may differ, yet the basic grieving process is the same.

Normally, people go through five stages of bereavement:

DENIAL: During this stage, we may refuse to accept that the loss has actually taken place. Sometimes we may play down the impact and convince ourselves the loss is reversible. Often people remain in the Denial stage, repress their feelings and carry on as normal for a while, until the unresolved feelings get triggered. June's case is an example of this.

ANGER: We may feel angry at ourselves or the other person for causing the loss or feeling of abandonment.

BARGAINING: We begin to have second thoughts and wonder, "Would he come back if...?"

DEPRESSION: We finally realize the loss is irreversible. We stop fighting the truth and become withdrawn and depressed.

ACCEPTANCE: We eventually face the reality of loss and are able to deal with it. Divorcees stop blaming themselves or others, put their lives together and start over again.

Bereavement is a vital process for a person to channel painful feelings and reclaim mental and emotional stability. However, a lot of courage and support is required to endure the agony of the process. Within a tight-knit expatriate community, people may try to suppress or cover up their grieving, for fear of gossip spreading. Sometimes people are tempted to take the easy way out and run away.

When people fail to grieve properly they are unlikely to let go of the past. They will live in a world of avoidance or denial until they are confronted with painful fact. After a divorce, if you haven't gone through the entire course of bereavement, you may hold onto the negative feelings, and eventually project them onto other relationships, which will cause another loss in the long run.

Being aware of the five stages of bereavement is half the battle toward recovery. When a person can finally acknowledge and accept a loss, he or she then is able to reinvest emotional energy in another relationship or task which is meaningful to him or her. Otherwise, he or she will remain in a world of anger, guilt, self-pity or helplessness. It is important for every person to examine his or her way of coping with loss. Choose the process of bereavement and not avoidance.

Being conscious of the bereavement process will help in confronting the next dilemma—to stay or to go home.

To leave or not to leave?

"I don't know where to go," Sandy cried. "I feel I have no home to return to."

After months of heated arguments, therapy and negotiation, Louis and Sandy finally came to a painful decision: divorce.

Sandy and Louis have been living abroad for over 12 years. With the divorce, Sandy finds herself stripped of her entire way of life. She has to move out of the company flat she'd considered home. Naturally, she no longer belongs to the bankers' wives' social circle. Trying to avoid painful old memories, she distances herself from former mutual friends.

Though Sandy was previously active with charity work, she can no longer afford the time. She is busy seeking employment and rebuilding her life. Her hands are full dealing with all the changes which come with divorce. Besides having to figure out who she is, she must also face the question of where she belongs.

In Sandy's case, she is in Taiwan because of Louis's career. After so many years there, the place is very much her home. Yet after the divorce there is no specific reason for her to remain. In many countries, a divorced unemployed foreigner will automatically lose their resident status. Thus, for Sandy to stay means finding her own career, both to support herself and to provide her with a visa.

Although Sandy receives a reasonable amount of maintenance, the idea of relying on someone who doesn't want to share her life makes her feels degraded and dependent. Therefore, finding a job is also an issue of self-esteem.

Yet when it comes to employment, she faces barriers because of her limited Chinese, and without specific marketable skills she may find herself unemployable. This makes it difficult to re-establish herself as an independent entity.

"I would be better off leaving Taiwan to have a fresh start."

Going home for Sandy seems like a natural move. But where is home for her? Being away from her native Belgium for so many years, she has grown apart from friends and places she once felt she belonged to. Furthermore, she and Louis have always lived in company flats, which leaves her not even a room she can call home. Sandy feels she has no "home" to return to anymore.

Even though Belgium was Sandy's native land, upon returning she would have to readjust, re-establish a social network and go through reverse cultural shock. All these can be overwhelming, on top of the emotional and other personal changes caused by the divorce. Also, she feels forced by circumstances into leaving. She may end up resenting the move to Belgium as much as the divorce.

Adjustment to divorce is hard enough by itself. An immediate move can cause additional commotion. If possible, people should limit the changes made at one time. Allow time to adjust to life without a partner or to being a single parent. Running away will not cure the pain, but may compound it even more.

Weigh the pros and cons of remaining abroad or returning home. Do not try to make a life-long decision during the immediate post-divorce stage. After all, once you can cope with the change and gradually rebuild your life your outlook will be different. Then is the right time for making long-term plans.

On the other hand, if you choose to go home you should reserve some emotional space. Do not feel obligated to report or share with people if you don't want to or aren't ready. Gently tell people that you need time to sort things out. Sometimes other's comments or criticism towards the former spouse will only add to the pain and confusion. Support from friends or relatives can be very helpful, but you need to select the ones who suit you.

Expatriate divorcees, especially non-breadwinners, obviously will face more changes. Returning home immediately should be treated as an option rather than a must if the situation allows.

Divorce can be a long and painful process. Even when divorce is final individuals still need a lot of time—up to two years—to adjust and cope with the changes. Most importantly, they need time to heal.

DEATH ON THE ROAD

The ultimate separation is, of course, death. The trauma caused by loss of a family member can be compounded when living overseas. Relatives, who would normally provide support, will be far away. The sudden loneliness of being left without a spouse, parent or child while living abroad can make those who remain feel helpless, abandoned and out of control.

Extra adjustments are necessary for an expatriate family when one member has passed away. Particularly when the deceased is the family breadwinner, death can mean not only a sudden adjustment to life without him or her; it may also mean loss of financial support, housing and other benefits, visa status and, especially, loss of the reason for being in that country in the first place. Thus the remaining family members are also faced with the decision of whether or not to move at short notice back to the home country.

An ever-present worry for expatriates or any family in which one member travels frequently is that an accident may occur while he or she is far away. The surviving spouse will be left feeling especially helpless or even guilty. When there are children left behind, the impact of the loss and so many adjustments can be too much for a parent to handle. The adult, already hurting and confused, may be at a loss how to tell the child.

> *"I don't know what to say to my daughter. Whenever she asks why her Daddy hasn't returned, I feel so terrible for her," Jane sobbed. "How can I help her understand? I hardly understand myself!"*

Jane's husband, a frequent traveler, died in a car accident during a business trip three months ago. He is survived by his wife and their three-year-old daughter, Betty.

A widowed parent like Jane faces the difficulty of talking to his or her child about the death of a parent. They don't know how much a child can understand, whether telling the truth is appropriate, or if it is better to cover it up until the child is older. Such questions cause the remaining parent confusion and delay in handling this important issue.

The most frequent and obvious question is:

SHOULD I TELL THE TRUTH TO MY CHILD ABOUT THE DEATH OF HIS OR HER LOVED ONE?

Telling the truth to children is important and inevitable. It will help both the remaining parent and the children to acknowledge the irreversible reality. This allows them all to grieve and move on with life. This holds true, whether the deceased is a parent, grandparent or other loved one.

However, before parents can tell the truth to their children they have to realize that a child's understanding of the concept of death varies with age.

Children under two years old appear to have no concept of death, although they do react to the absence of a significant individual and to the feelings of those around them. From ages two to five, children usually view death as a familiar condition like sleep. They don't believe the condition to be permanent. At age five, most children have some sense of the permanence of death, yet their thinking is selective. The idea that everybody, including children, has to die is not understood. Not until nine years of age can children normally understand the final, irreversibility of death.

Since Jane's daughter Betty is only three, it is very difficult for her to understand why her Daddy is not returning after a period of absence. For her, things may disappear, but they always return, just as Daddy always did after a trip.

In telling the truth to the child, certain explanations of death should be avoided because of the potential for misunderstanding. Adults should resist the temptation to describe death as a "long sleep", "long journey" or that "God took him." These answers may create negative associations with sleep, travel or God.

The child might believe that if she goes to sleep, she will never wake up. This will cause sleep disturbances, such as nightmares and waking up in the middle of the night. Similarly, a child might fear repeat abandonment by the remaining parent during any physical separation. Anger and resentment may result from literally believing that God has taken away her loved one. God should not be blamed, but rather, depending on the family's beliefs, seen as receiving the departed one and offering comfort to the living.

Another question often asked is:

HOW CAN I TELL MY CHILD SO THAT SHE OR HE CAN UNDERSTAND?

When adults try to explain death to children, they should employ simplified language which relates to the child's world. Providing daily life examples of things the deceased cannot do will give a child a better understanding of death. For example: "Daddy can't read to you anymore." If necessary, use drawings, play acting or puppets to get the meaning across to the child. It would also be helpful to ask the child to use his or her words to explain what death is. This way, parents can get a clearer picture of how their child views death and help correct the concept if necessary.

SHOULD I SHARE MY GRIEF WITH MY CHILDREN?

Sometimes surviving parents purposely hide their own feelings, thinking they are protecting their children from further alarm or sadness. However, no matter how hard one tries, it is inevitable that the children will sense it.

Both parent and children should directly display their feelings. This will enable them to find mutual support and grow closer as a family. It will also encourage the child to voice their questions and fears; for example, what caused the death, or whether the child or the other parent will now die. Such questions should be dealt with openly and honestly.

Helping young children through bereavement is far more difficult than helping adults. Adults must understand and accept that children don't necessarily grieve the same way as grown-ups. Adults should not get angry when a child doesn't cry or express sadness in the same way they do.

Use concrete data instead of philosophical notions to explain death. Teach them that the attachment with the dead parent is ended and reaffirm that the surviving one will continue to care for them. Children, just like adults, need time to accept the bitter reality of death in the family.

Truth hurts, but it also heals. When a family has suffered a loss, whether through death or divorce, parents must openly share their grief with their children. After all, this is a time when each person needs all the love and comfort he or she can get. With mutual support, they can go on with life and face the future together.

Chapter 9

The expatriate underclass

THE FORGOTTEN CLASS

WHEN REFERRING TO expatriates, the common understanding is that of business people, journalists, professional teachers and diplomats, all relatively well off, enjoying comfortable lifestyles, frequent travel, and having every need paid for. On a lower economic level, we think of language tutors, exchange students, artists, researchers, self-imposed exiles, and transients working their way around the world. But in many, if not most, countries, all the above combined account for less than half of the foreign population.

We usually don't refer to foreign guest workers and migrant laborers as expatriates. But that is indeed what they are, sharing many of the same goals, advantages and difficulties as those in more privileged positions.

From Germany to Kuwait to Taiwan, foreign workers build our buildings and clean our houses. Most leave home for economic reasons; not much different than a banking executive going abroad to further his career. Some take their families; most don't. They, too, are subject to most of the problems referred to in this book: from culture shock to isolation to problems of separation.

One group of the expatriate underclass, though, has its own special problems to compound all the others. From the Far East to the Middle East, one finds women from Third World Asian countries—especially the Philippines, Thailand, Indonesia, Bangladesh and Sri Lanka—who left home and family behind to work as house servants. Some are from poor families, but many are educated, professional women who find they can earn more cleaning house in a foreign country than they can as a teacher, nurse or architect back home. They go abroad to save up money for their families' sakes for years at a time and often only return when immigration regulations require them to.

These lower-class "astronauts" inhabit the luxurious homes of the wealthy and middle class in the host countries, and, of course, of nearly every professional-level expatriate. Yet their pay is meager, most of it sent home. and their status in society is very low. Most work in isolation six or seven days a week—serving a family, but not being a part of it—and are restricted from going out except on errands or during their legally mandated time off (and often not even then).

This is not to paint an entirely gloomy picture of a foreign maid's life. Like everyone else, she learns to adapt and make the best out of it. For most, the benefits received far outweigh the disadvantages. But sometimes a woman in such a position can lose sight of what or whom she is working for—is it her employer, her family, or herself?

STRANGERS IN TWO LANDS

Joyce choked with tears. "I wipe their babies' bottoms, but I don't belong to the family I work with. I also don't feel I belong to my own family, who I maybe see once a year. What am I working so hard for?"

Joyce, 33 years old, is married with two children. She came to Hong Kong four years ago as a domestic helper. She has just returned from two weeks home in the Philippines. Since returning she has been feeling depressed and unmotivated.

According to Joyce, being home was like living in a bad dream. She had given up her profession as a teacher and come to Hong Kong for the sake of family finances. With her husband's initial support she fully accepted the long-distance separation from those she loves. After sacrificing so much for her family, she had hoped for some love and support in return.

However, once home she realized that her husband was unappreciative. Right away he showed his disappointment at not receiving all the items he had requested her to bring for him. Her children have grown and get along without her. Her parents, siblings and relatives didn't hesitate to tell her all their problems, and hold their hands out to the "rich" returnee. Overwhelmed with others' needs and troubles, Joyce found it difficult to open herself to them, since no one thought she had any complaints. After all, she dressed well and appeared to be financially comfortable. "No one ever stopped to ask how I feel," Joyce said.

Back in Hong Kong she finds herself living and working intimately with the host family, yet she cannot be part of it. Even though she feels that her employers are kind and sympathetic, she cannot burden them with her problems. Required to perform and remain cheerful on the job, Joyce is busy meeting the needs of the employer's household. Once again her own needs have to be pushed aside, if not swallowed.

Domestic servants, like other expatriates who leave their families behind and come to a foreign land for financial advantage, are bound to sacrifice some of their personal interests or needs. The separation from her family can be devastating. Normally, the trauma can be lessened through phone calls, visits, and local support and activities.

However, Filipina domestic helpers are without the financial privileges that other expatriates have, and their communication with family mostly depends on brief calls and text messages. Frequent travel home is out of the question. Usually they return for only two to three weeks every two years.

One way for expatriates to deal with homesickness and loneliness is to make outside contacts. Yet most expatriate domestic helpers start working in the morning and don't finish until whatever hour their employers require. By then it may be bedtime. They are practically on-call 24 hours a day. It is easy to feel confined and trapped in such a situation. The lack of personal space and the feeling of being at the mercy of her employers, as well as a maid's low status in society, can cause a person to completely lose her identity.

Joyce is caught in a bind between duty and personal needs. Whether she stays in Hong Kong or returns home, she has something to lose, either emotionally or financially.

Returning home is not the immediate solution for someone in Joyce's situation. Since she came to Hong Kong for practical financial reasons, if she drops everything to run home, she will inevitably feel guilt and face resentment from her family.

The lack of direct emotional support from family and employer can create a lonely and difficult situation. In order to deal with the situation more effectively, it is important to reach out to friends as well as build one's own inner strength. Of most importance is that she honestly, and without fear, shares her feelings with the people back home, including anger and disappointment. This will eventually result in greater closeness and support.

A woman like Joyce should avoid treating herself as a martyr who must sacrifice all pleasures. Setting some personal goals will give her a sense of direction; for example, setting aside part of her salary to open her own business in the future back home. Taking up new skills or interests during days off can make life more pleasant. Most of all, such a person needs to put a time limit on her overseas work so that she knows what she is heading toward and will have a better perspective on her future.

Chapter 10

Going home

WHEN ONE PARTNER WANTS TO GO HOME

AFTER A FEW years of living overseas, many couples find themselves in the position where one spouse wants to move back home and the other doesn't. This is often because one—often the wife—had to give up her career, due to lack of opportunities in the new place. The decision is usually made willingly and for the sake of the family. However, after the novelty of living abroad wears off, many such women feel frustration and loss of identity.

Meanwhile, many men, or working women, are reluctant to give up the excitement, status and perks they receive in their overseas posting. This conflict of interests is one of the most common, and most difficult, causes of marital tension and heartbreak among expatriates. It must be dealt with extremely sensitively by both partners.

> Marianne was angry. "I'm tired of you avoiding the subject of moving back to Boston. Every time I bring it up, you joke about it and totally ignore my feelings."

> "Look, I just don't want to fight, dear. Of course I care about your feelings," Bob said.

Marianne is threatening to leave her husband Bob unless they move back to the United States at the end of his current contract.

Bob and Marianne have been married for ten years and have one child. The family moved to Singapore five years ago, when Bob's bank sent him to be in charge of their Southeast Asian branch headquarters. He feels comfortable and settled there. But his wife had to give up her profession as a nurse when they moved abroad and has never felt totally satisfied living in Singapore.

As Bob's third term contract comes up for renewal Marianne has started pressuring him to transfer back home, which he had promised to do a few years back. Until now, both have believed that because Bob is the breadwinner, he is also the decision-maker. Marianne is beginning to question that. The tension between them is apparent.

For Marianne the luxurious lifestyle and travel were attractive for a while but they could not eliminate her dissatisfaction at being unable to pursue her own goals. She makes frequent trips home to be with friends and family as her way of dealing with the frustration of living in Asia. "The money is good, but I don't want to grow old here," claims Marianne. Secretly she counts the days to move back home.

However, for Bob the idea of returning home is dreadful. He enjoys his little "empire" in Singapore.

With tremendous responsibility and decision-making power, Bob gains a great sense of importance from being "somebody" among his staff and colleagues. On top of this, he enjoys all the expatriate perks and privileges, such as club membership and the company yacht, which make his life very charming.

For many expatriates, the fear of returning home can be overwhelming. Expatriate communities the world over are filled with people who "came for two years" but stayed for twenty.

After investing several years of his life in Singapore building up the present situation, going back seems like a step down. Trading in a prominent, powerful position in business and society to become just another suit back in the home office, living an "average" middle-class existence, would be like going backwards in life. Therefore, Bob has extended his original two-year contract several times.

Bob assumes that Marianne brings up the subject of returning to Boston out of moodiness and occasional home-sickness. He tries to avoid the subject, thinking she will soon forget it. This time around, when she is actually threatening to leave him, it took him by surprise. He believes that his wife's reaction is out of proportion. He feels that she is unap-preciative of what she has in Singapore, that she thinks only of herself and little of his career prospects.

Marianne, on the other hand, accuses Bob of being selfish, only thinking of his own needs and ambitions and totally disregarding hers. She feels hurt, angry and taken for granted. Even though they generally have a good marriage she cannot see herself continuing to be treated in this way. She feels she has given up so much for him. She believes she has a perfect right to ask him to do something for her—that is, to move back home to the United States.

In this situation, there is no "right" or "wrong" side.

Their problem is a lack of honest and direct communica-tion. When the couple avoids fighting, "to keep the peace", they only make the situation worse.

Often a couple tries to avoid arguments at all costs. But in fact, fights can be good, healthy, and even necessary. Arguing can give people a chance to vent their frustration as well as to uncover misunderstandings or assumptions between them. In Bob and Marianne's case, if things had been clarified much earlier, they might not have built up to the point of explosion.

If one partner's dream is being fulfilled at the expense of their spouse's needs and desires, inevitably a crisis will result. A couple must be careful not to give precedence to the partner who happens to make more money. Unfortunately, this is usually the case, and any expatriate couple must examine whether they are allowing money alone to guide their lives.

Similarly, each should not swallow his or her objections to a major decision which affects both people equally.

Genuine agreement must be reached in order for everyone to be satisfied. Afterwards, frequent evaluations of the situation and open discussion of each other's feelings can help to prevent bitterness or resentment from building up.

Is going home the right decision?

"I've had it with this place," Stanley said. "Things are too crazy here. I really cannot stay and keep my sanity."

Stanley and his wife Karen, both teachers in their mid-thirties, have been living in Jakarta for six years. They have made plans to leave Indonesia at the end of the school term. However, as the time nears, Stanley has become agitated, tense and depressed.

"On the other hand, I don't know what's wrong with me. I'm starting to wonder whether I've made the

right decision," he said. "Just thinking about all the things we have to do before leaving is tiring. I have no energy these days. Am I going through midlife crisis?"

Stanley is confused by his own reaction and doesn't know how to deal with it.

His behavior is an anxiety reaction towards imminent change. The decision which will affect both him and his family puts tremendous pressure on him to make it "right". However, people in such a state easily feel confused and doubt their ability to make sound judgments.

Stanley claims that both he and Karen are fed up with the lifestyle in Jakarta and are willing to give up what they have to return home. Yet after years of settling into one place, the thought of moving is understandably quite stressful.

They came to Indonesia, excited about moving halfway around the world, in their late twenties. But when people reach their mid-thirties many tend to be less adventurous than before. Stability and security assume greater importance. Inevitably more things will be taken into consideration before making another big move.

As much as he wants to get out of Jakarta and go back home, he is also worried about "starting all over again". The opportunities for teachers back home are few and not so well paid as his job in Indonesia. The idea of facing the tight job market puts his fragile confidence on trial. Under such circumstances, it is not uncommon for second thoughts to arise. The idea of staying put in a familiar and comfortable environment suddenly seems attractive.

Giving up all the things he spent years building up is frightening and painful. He begins to question his own values. "My dislike of the lifestyle: is it a good enough reason for me to give up so much?" he puzzled. He seems to have lost sight of what originally caused him to decide to leave.

Many people about to give up or lose something familiar may suddenly become afraid to let go. Stanley even glamorizes things that used to annoy him. Crowds become stimulating rather than annoying. Busy streets full of hawkers and pedicabs seem lively compared with the sedate suburbs back home.

When faced with a dilemma like Stanley's, the first step is to objectively look into and evaluate the original motivations for change.

Stanley's major complaints are the lifestyle and the pollution of crowded, unattractive Jakarta. It is important to clarify whether the local environment is the major cause or whether there are other contributing factors. Personal or marital problems, or general inability to manage money or to make friends, might have led to his dissatisfaction. If that is the case, moving is not the cure for the problem.

Once the motive is clear, the next step is to come to a real decision. The family should first prioritize their life in terms of definable issues, such as current and future finance, career for both partners, social life for all family members, schooling for children, and so on. Then they can evaluate whether they are willing, or can afford, to give up one thing to pursue the other.

For example, it may be in an individual's interest to move to a place with a cleaner environment and better lifestyle but with lesser career prospects. However, other individuals may put other factors, such as finances, at the top of the list and delay their plans.

Generally when expatriates go abroad, it is for better career opportunities and financial reward. When coming to a major decision like relocation, finance can become a stumbling block and overrule everything. Thus, it is important to review the overall situation and list all the pros and cons before the final decision is made.

IDENTITY INFLATION, PART II

The decision has been made. Perhaps not by you. But it is time to go back to the home country.

A great number of expatriates are quite reluctant to return, even if there is a job and a house waiting for them. Almost everyone knows someone who quit their company or even switched careers in order to stay abroad. They realize that expat life is not just about money. Living overseas changes a person; it can be quite hard to go home again.

After nine years abroad, Phillip's company has offered to transfer him back to the home office, with commensurate promotion within the company.

"It's an attractive offer. But at the same time, it feels like a big step down."

Returning home can have pleasant connotations for most expatriates. They look forward to a triumphant return, flush with success and prestige that they can display to their fellow countrymen and colleagues. However, when the moment arrives, it is easy to feel exactly the opposite. Such a letdown is a product of Identity Inflation.

Identity Inflation, discussed in Chapter Two, means an individual's sense of identity has in certain respects been blown out of proportion. When placed back in the old environment, he no longer feels the same about himself nor do people perceive him as in the past. The person feels deflated in importance and self-worth.

Identity inflation can lead to identity crisis. The returnee loses his or her uniqueness as an expatriate and their seemingly lofty, powerful position in business and society. Back in the home country, he no longer stands out from the crowd. At work he is surrounded by other people just like him.

To a certain degree, a returned expat is even treated like an outsider. After all, he's been out of circulation and isn't familiar with day-to-day office politics. Such a person may end up feeling more out of place than when he was a foreigner in another country.

The most difficult problem to overcome is when colleagues don't look upon overseas experience with the proper respect. To many homebound colleagues, foreign experience is irrelevant or of "lower" standard. If people ever acknowledge it, it is more out of curiosity than anything else. A person like Phillip knows this, and does not look forward to dealing with it.

Above all, the impending change of lifestyle can cause a major degree of identity *de*flation. From living on an expatriate package, including free luxury housing, maids, paid home leave, paid private education for the children, he is going back to living in the suburbs and driving his own car.

Change in identity is an inevitable part of returning home. But the anxiety that it causes should not interfere with a person's decision to go. After all, the decision to return home was a choice arrived at presumably for valid reasons.

Once a decision is made, it should be stuck to. Anxiety and stress prior to any change are unavoidable. But if priorities are clearly defined and chosen, an individual can move into the future, confident that the decision was the right one.

RETIRING BACK HOME

Returning to the home country is not just an issue for people on temporary foreign assignment or unhappy with living overseas. Even those who have worked contentedly for twenty, thirty or more years in a foreign country must face the decision of where to go when they retire.

It is surprising how few long-term expatriates retire in the country in which they made their home and career for so many years. This is a time of life when people face many changes. Most would prefer to avoid risks or upheaval. For that reason, the decision about where to retire should not be taken lightly.

"I always thought of retirement as a reward for people who've worked hard all their lives," George said. "I don't know why I'm not at all thrilled when it comes to my turn. "

George, 63, has been living in Hong Kong with his family for the last 24 years and will retire in six months. He is facing a great deal of anxiety about his retirement and especially the idea of moving back home to Australia.

Retirement has different meanings to different individuals. Some people can't wait to retire so that they can be free from responsibility and do what they want. But for others retirement means "old age", redundancy and uselessness.

People approaching retirement age face both emotional and identity changes. For expatriates it has an even greater impact, especially if they have lived abroad for some time and are contemplating settling back in their home country. Returning "home" seems the natural and logical step, but it can heighten the adjustment difficulties of retirement.

Retirement can signify a loss of identity for a career person. He or she has worked for many years to reach where they are. Their position and achievement reinforce self-worth and identity. Yet, when a person retires in a place halfway around the world from where they have made their career and established their reputation, self-identity will be stripped away and remain only a memory. This can be a big blow to the ego.

For George, the loss is being anticipated with a great deal of resistance. "I'll be just like any old retiree with no clear sense of purpose in life anymore." Another adjustment George faces is imminent change of environment. He expresses a vague fear of moving back to Australia, even though he has planned the move for three years. He and his wife have already bought a house there and begun shipping their goods. George's fear is legitimate. After all, he will be relocating to a place they call "home", but which he is no longer familiar with. Though he realizes he will have to go through some adjustment and readaptation, the whole idea is frightening and exhausting. "I'm at the age where I don't want to take risks or make drastic changes," he said.

The retirement will also call for changes in the marital relationship. George's wife Miriam is used to being actively involved with her own interests and social groups while George was at the office. With George no longer working they are bound to spend much more time together. This will provoke responses on both sides. For George, accustomed to a structured working lifestyle, the sudden change of having time on his hands may bring out some frustration. Meanwhile, Miriam may find her life being intruded upon and restricted with her husband around so often.

This situation will be even more pronounced once they relocate. They leave behind their group of friends built up over 24 years, to return "home" where they have little social support. The few friends they maintained contact with in Australia over the years may not be able to share their experiences or understand what they are going through. Naturally, both George and Miriam will turn to each other for support. This can create a mutual dependency, which they both need and resent at the same time. For couples who have a good relationship the situation will be nurturing, but for others it may become a breeding ground for conflicts.

Expatriate retirees need to evaluate whether relocating is suitable for them. Usually it is considered only natural for someone at the end of their career to retire to the country they came from. But after such a long time away, "back home" may feel just as alien as any foreign country.

Those who will relocate to the home country need to prepare themselves for reverse cultural shock (see below). They should not take things for granted or expect to just fit right in. They need to be patient with themselves and allow time to refamiliarize with the old environment.

Retirement brings changes to everyone's life. It is very much up to individuals to minimize the difficulties in adjusting to this transitional period. Accepting the inevitable changes is essential. Allow time to get used to a life without work deadlines or targets. It will be a new challenge to manage one's own time. Make efforts to develop new interests as well as mutual interests with spouse and friends. After retirement, it is important to maintain a balanced and healthy lifestyle with strong social support.

Retirement needn't be dreaded or feared, nor need it become a life of boredom and exile. By considering all the available options, and choosing the one that feels right, it can be a welcome beginning to a new chapter of your life.

REVERSE CULTURAL SHOCK

Returning to the homeland involves more than packing and farewell parties. Psychological preparation for re-entering the home country is just as important. However, the issue of "reverse cultural shock" is often overlooked by returning individuals and families.

Stanley and his wife Karen, described earlier, have just spent six years in a conservative, predominantly Muslim country.

Moving back to their native Scotland is obviously going to be something of a shock. But because it is "home", they do not anticipate the adjustments they will have to undergo to fit back in to their chilly northern European society.

Returning home after an extended stay abroad is both exciting and stressful. After all the physical and mental strain of packing, shipping, tying up loose ends and leaving, one looks forward to arriving and quickly settling down in a comfortable, familiar environment. In actual fact, once they have returned home the hard part has just begun, something which takes most returning expatriates by surprise.

Reverse cultural shock is actually more difficult to deal with than the original cultural shock experienced when entering a new land. This is because most people don't anticipate the need for adjustment when returning to their home country.

In order to understand reverse cultural shock a person needs to remember what they actually went through in the initial cultural shock when entering a foreign country:

ELATION: Usually during the first several weeks in a new culture everything is fresh and new. A newcomer feels excited and elated.

HOMESICKNESS: When the excitement wears off, a person is confronted with daily life in the new society, where everything can be quite different from back home. Some people refuse to adapt to the new culture, associating only with their own crowd and remaining aloof from the local population.

TRANSFORMATION: After about nine months, they feel more familiar with the environment and begin to see the good side of the new culture. They gradually adopt the new ways of living. Sometimes people in this stage may go to another extreme, rejecting their own culture and viewing everything back home as "unsophisticated" or not as attractive.

ACCULTURATION: When people learn how to integrate the "old" and "new", they can fully appreciate their own origin as well as the new culture.

When expatriates relocate back home after having been away for a long time, they are likely to experience similar stages of acculturation. This is called "reverse cultural shock":

ELATION: Welcomed back by long-missed family members and friends makes a returnee feel secure, knowing this is his or her "real" home. They can enjoy driving on a big wide road or strolling along the street without pushing through crowds. Things seem so pleasant and calm at home. Such feelings remain for the first several days or weeks.

RE-ENTRY SHOCK: Fitting right in to the home circle and returning to "normal" life doesn't happen overnight. The fact is, a recent returnee will feel very different from everyone around. This will make him or her feel delighted and special on the one hand, but on the other it brings confusion and a sense of isolation.

For example, Stanley is very eager to point out that "I've just returned from five years overseas." By doing so he knows he can draw others' attention and reassures himself that he is unique, interesting and different. It's easy to overdo it, though. Even cashiers and waiters are not exempt from his frequent asides that, "Ha ha. I forgot that's how they do things here."

Family and friends will demonstrate interest in the returnee's adventures, anecdotes and little comparative comments, though their attention spans seem surprisingly short. At a family dinner, Stanley finds that the relatives are not nearly as fascinated at hearing about the night bazaars and morning prayer calls in Jakarta, as they are in hearing Auntie Beatrice from Inverness describe Uncle Ralph's prostate operation.

To many returnees, this apparent disinterest is a great surprise. It is also a disappointment that leads to feeling disoriented and isolated.

In some cases returned expatriates carry their feeling of being special too far. They may tend to pick on friends and people in general for being unsophisticated or narrowminded about the world. They will repeatedly draw comparisons between home and the foreign country. For example, saying at restaurants, "This isn't real Chinese food," or constantly remarking, "You know how cheap that would be back in Indonesia?"

Such commentary will eventually annoy and bore others, who will take it as showing off. These actions will keep people at a distance and make it difficult to readjust to the old circle. Most people are oblivious to whatever changes may have gone on inside a person from living abroad. For the most part, friends and family believe that you still think and act exactly the way they do, as if you'd never left. The returnee may therefore feel inhibited from saying or doing anything that could appear "show-offy". He or she may be reluctant to discuss any feelings of disappointment or disorientation at being back, for fear nobody will understand.

METAMORPHOSIS: The former expatriate literally has to shed one skin for another. They are in the transitional process of losing their expatriate identity, yet without having totally re-established a new sense of identity for themselves.

Faced with the day-to-day routine, they often begin to long for the favorable lifestyle once enjoyed in the foreign land. The travel, climate, servants, cultural experiences, mingling with an international group of expatriates, as well as the social status and the special treatment they were accustomed to are sorely missed. A returnee may begin to think back to the good old days. He or she may even refuse or resent readjustment to the lifestyle of the home country.

Such a phenomenon is often reinforced by having lost touch with the trends, fashions, popular music and television, and local politics back home. Such disorientation can easily make people lose their balance and feel stupid, vulnerable and alienated. It can lead individuals to conclude that returning was a bad choice.

READAPTATION TO HOME CULTURE: Given time, returned expatriates will re-familiarize themselves with the home environment and appreciate what is there. They finally accept what they have given up in the foreign society and are happy to settle down at home.

Readaptation is a gradual process rather than a distinct stage that a person goes through. It will not take place until the individual has passed through the first three stages and is able to understand what is going through his or her own mind.

Understanding the stages of reacculturation does not necessarily make it easier or pleasant to endure. However, reminding yourself when things seem tough that, after all, what you are going through is only normal, is the best—and only—way to deal with reverse cultural shock. It is vital to avoid becoming too skeptical or cynical about the return home and not to run back overseas before giving yourself and family members a chance to cope with the re-entry.

Individuals returning from foreign places need time to readjust and confront their reverse cultural shock. Inevitably, an ex-expatriate will fit back in to the home environment. but he or she always will be a different individual because of their unique experience.

Returnees need to be highly sensitive and not impose their views on others who may not have had the privilege to experience or understand what they had overseas. It is important to resist holding oneself above others and remind oneself not to loudly compare one society to the other.

Reverse cultural shock comes as a painful surprise. Eventually the discomfort and negative feelings will dissipate, and the returnee will fit in and feel comfortable back home. It takes time, as little as six months or as long as two years, before the last vestiges of reverse cultural shock fade away. As long as a returnee is prepared to go through re-acculturation, and is sensitive to himself or herself and to those around, he or she can make the adjustment less painful for everyone concerned.

Chapter 11

Happily ever after

HOME IS WHERE YOUR FAMILY IS

NO MATTER WHAT joys and pitfalls you may encounter in a foreign country—at work, in social settings, or out on the street—at the end of each day you always go home. Home in this case means the apartment, house, hotel, bungalow or tent you live in now. Whether temporary or long-term, it is still home for you and your family.

If you do not have a happy family life, no number of exciting outside experiences or outstanding accomplishments will change the situation. On the other hand, a happy home life will enable you to face difficulties and challenges on the outside much more easily. Whether you live abroad or if you've never left your home town, a happy home is the catalyst for a happy life.

For most people, marriage or another form of committed relationship is either a reality or a goal. Thus, a happy home life, and a satisfying life in general, both depend quite a bit on the success of the relationship.

THE CHOICE IS YOURS

Marriage is a joyous, fulfilling union for most couples, but for others it can be a meaningless and exploitative trap.

A good marriage doesn't come effortlessly. It requires work and nurturing from both partners. Each must be willing to communicate, learn to resolve conflicts and accept differences.

Every couple has the choice either to build a lifelong happy marriage for themselves or to become the victims of their marriage. What will be your choice?

In the following pages we will look at aspects of building and maintaining a happy, successful marriage, so that a couple, meaning both partners equally, can flourish, grow and enjoy, no matter where in this world they go.

Avoiding misconceptions
before marriage

When two people decide to get married, a lot of attention is paid to preparations for the wedding, the honeymoon, combining households, and so on. But in preparing psychologically for marriage, many people are not nearly so thorough.

It is common to hear engaged or newlywed couples declare: "Whatever differences we have will be resolved by love." This is a sweet sentiment, reinforced by popular songs and movies, but unfortunately it is not always true.

Marriage is the union of two people, with different personalities, habits and beliefs. It is living together, sharing both joys and responsibilities, triumphs and disappointments, the great and the trivial. Since no two people are exactly alike and no one person should be subservient to another, differences are bound to arise.

Most marital tension comes from unspoken assumptions and not knowing how to resolve conflicts. If an engaged couple reveals their assumptions about one another and about married life, and they learn how to resolve differences before they are married, then it is more likely that love will indeed help them to eliminate unpleasant feelings after their marriage.

Tom and Janet are engaged to be married.

"We're going to have a kid right away," Tom said.

"Wait a minute. Where did you get that idea? I don't think I want kids for at least three years," Janet declared.

These statements were made during a premarital counseling session. Luckily, Tom and Janet were able to discover and resolve their differences on this and other issues before marriage.

Most couples like Tom and Janet talk for countless hours during the courtship period and believe they know each other well. Most don't realize they have built up expectations toward the potential spouse.

During courtship, couples formulate a certain pattern of communicating with each other. While dating, it is only natural to cover our embarrassing habits, flaws and temperaments. Yet once married, all these flaws or differences are exposed during daily encounters and can consequently lead to tension and arguments.

"It will all work out after we're married."
"It doesn't really bother me, I'm sure I'll get used to it."

These are myths people carry into marriage. Differences between two individuals are unavoidable. Such points of potential conflict do not disappear by magic, nor will time necessarily change anything. Unless the differences, assumptions and expectations are dealt with or negotiated, they will turn into disappointments, dismay and disharmony in the marriage.

Quite often we hear one spouse say, "He or she changed so much after we got married." Usually the fact is, he or she didn't change, they are just being themselves.

Before committing oneself to a lifetime partnership, it is important to look into areas that may trigger potential conflicts. Some of these areas may seem to be petty, yet can place a couple in a constant tug of war in which mutual understanding and agreement cannot be reached.

LIVING ARRANGEMENTS: Where a couple will live after marriage, and the proximity to parents and in-laws, has a direct impact on career opportunities, social life and family support. If either side is unsatisfied with the arrangement it will be difficult to create a loving and harmonious atmosphere at home.

CHILDREN: Many people put little thought into the enormous impact children can have on a newlywed couple. Children affect a couple's intimacy, social life, finances, career plans, and other life priorities. An engaged couple must reach a mutual understanding and agreement on whether to have children, when, and how many. This is crucial, since any hidden frustration or resentments on this matter will most likely be passed on to the children.

The business of child rearing also needs to be considered carefully. Whether the mother will return to work and how the children will be disciplined and trained should be discussed before the baby comes. Differences in opinion over child raising often lead to tremendous conflict and argument, causing not only bad feelings between the parents, but also confusion in the child.

FINANCE: Money is always a sensitive issue within a marriage. It can be a source of competition or manipulation in a battle for control and power. It is important for the prospective bride and groom to clearly discuss future financial arrangements and the way they view money. Other questions they should ask themselves are: How will financial decisions be made? Will the both husband and wife work? Full time or part time? Who will be in charge of family budgeting? How does each feel about the issues of credit and debt? Or about receiving money from parents?

COMMUNICATION: It is important that a couple learn how to share their feelings and how to work through disagreements prior to and after the wedding. Honest and direct communication will provide strength for couples to withstand and resolve differences. An unhealthy pattern of communication can cause mistrust and destruction in a marriage.

Other important areas for discussion include religion, attitudes toward in-laws and friends, diet and hygiene.

All these areas need to be discussed and explored at least six months before the actual wedding. However, it is easy to lose our objectivity when it comes to issues that directly reflect our views and beliefs. It is helpful to seek premarital counseling from a supportive clergyman or counselor.

Premarital counseling is a short-term process which usually requires about six to seven sessions. Through this the bride and groom-to-be will have an opportunity to evaluate their views and expectations of marriage as well as prepare themselves for a realistic way of handling future marital issues.

HOW TO STAY HAPPILY MARRIED

Eliminating misconceptions before marriage does not prevent new ones from arising afterwards.

There are a lot of myths about marriage. For example: "After several years, marriage is bound to become less exciting, routine and dull." This is only true if you're willing to settle for a merely mediocre marriage, which is then what you'll get.

Marriage is like a living plant which constantly needs water, fertilizer and, most of all, care. The longer you are married, the more work you have to put in to keep the marriage flourishing.

Following are several questions a therapist routinely asks to evaluate the state of a marriage. These will give you some guidelines in evaluating your own state of marital or relationship satisfaction.

HOW MUCH TIME DO YOU SPEND WITH YOUR SPOUSE?

"Plenty," say many couples. However, when we get down to it, time that couples spend together exclusively for intimacy and expression of feelings towards each other is very limited. Such time can be viewed in a hierarchy. Is the time you spend with your spouse:

High-quality time: attentive and intimate, either verbally or non-verbally communicating with each other without outside distractions?

Medium-quality time: more business-like, voicing each other's views about children, in-laws, other family issues or work?

Low-quality time: together within the same premises, but either one or both is occupied by chores, television, children or computer?

Special effort is required to create more high-quality time together when living in a distracting foreign environment.

WHAT KIND OF PRIORITY DO YOU GIVE YOUR PARTNER AS FAR AS TIME IS CONCERNED?

- Do you make time to be with your spouse no matter how busy you may be?

- Do you spend time with your spouse only when he or she asks?

- Are you sharing your leftover time with your spouse, only when you have no other things to do?

For many couples, priority is often given to children. For others, career and job come first. The only time they spend alone together is when they are in bed, half-asleep. The couple ends up with only leftover time for each other.

DO YOU ENJOY TALKING WITH YOUR SPOUSE AND SHARING YOUR THOUGHTS AND FEELINGS?

Many people will answer: "Of course I enjoy talking to my spouse" ...*but*... "I'm too busy," "Our children take up too much of my time," or "We don't seem to have much to talk about anymore."

Enjoying talking to and sharing your thoughts with your partner is the basic premise of a satisfying marriage. Couples need to identify what may be the possible causes that limit their talking and sharing. Does the busy lifestyle take away time that a couple share? Or does basic incompatibility make them create excuses to avoid communicating with each other?

HOW INTIMATE AND MEANINGFUL IS YOUR COMMUNICATION?

Couples often occupy the same house and bed but feel like strangers. They want to share and be intimate, but find themselves growing apart. They communicate ideas and facts but rarely share their personal feelings about each other. However, when open communication is established, couples will be free to share feelings and thoughts. Through this they increase mutual understanding which will enhance intimacy and the growth of their marriage.

DO YOU AND YOUR PARTNER AVOID INTIMACY?

Often couples work as a team to avoid intimacy without realizing it. For example, one partner may continuously keep him or herself busy at home or at work, while the spouse is absorbed by television, computer or hobbies. Superficially, both look quite content and peaceful without being bothered by each other. At the same time, the chance for closeness is being sabotaged.

How do you and your partner create intimacy?

Open communication is the way to maintain intimacy in a marriage. This means a willingness to share your honest feelings and thoughts as well as to listen to your partner. It means seeking ways to resolve conflicts rather than ignoring them. It means respecting each other's differences. It is a willingness to apologize or forgive and not dwell on past grievances.

Love and romance are important in a marriage, but they are not the only ingredients. To keep a marriage—and the original romance—alive, both partners need to have open communication and quality time together.

A happy marriage is not a matter of chance. You can make the choice for marital happiness, if both you and your spouse are willing to put in the work. In this way, you will enjoy a thriving marriage rather than become victims of a bad marriage.

OPEN COMMUNICATION

"She doesn't understand me," Joe said.

"He doesn't respond when I talk to him," said Sheila.

These are statements I hear often in my therapy room. At times people find they can't communicate with their spouse, who is supposed to be their most intimate partner in life. Often, attempts at communication end up in conflict.

"How can we communicate better and resolve conflicts?" many people ask. There are methods that can lead to more effective communication. provided genuine participation and practice are provided.

Before we can work on improving communication we have to understand what causes poor or miscommunication.

DENIAL: "Oh, no, it doesn't bother me," Sheila said. Meanwhile, inside she is thinking: "...but I'm really mad as hell!" When Joe stayed out a few nights in a row with his drinking buddies. Sheila felt angry and left out. But she denied her own feelings and hoped they would go away. However, unresolved feelings are often projected onto other marital issues. For example, she overly criticizes the way Joe dresses. If such feelings continue to be suppressed, it will snowball and cause general resentment between the couple.

EXPECTATION: "Why should I always have to explain?" Joe snapped. Joe returned home exhausted and expected to have some peace and quiet. But Sheila and the children all noisily demanded his attention. Joe became angry that his wife didn't understand his need and he yelled at her. Many people assume since they've lived so long with their spouse, he or she should be able to read their mind. When things don't turn out the way they expected they become angry or disappointed.

ASSUMPTION: "You already said enough," Sheila yelled. When Joe started to explain about the office open house, Sheila immediately assumed that Joe was trying to talk her out of going. She felt rejected and refused to listen. Sometimes couples find themselves communicating on different wavelengths. One or both listen only to what they want to hear. Before one partner can finish the message, the other has reacted to what they assume they heard.

AVOIDANCE: "Come on, you're just overreacting," Joe said. When Sheila complained that they never spend time alone, Joe brushed it aside. Sometimes people try to avoid the uncomfortable feelings roused by confrontation, by making jokes or changing the subject.

To enhance better communication, couples need to remove communication blocks by:

USING "I" MESSAGES: Avoid blaming your partner for your feelings. For example, "I am not happy about how you relate to my friends," instead of "You made me angry and embarrassed!" By using "I" messages you take responsibility for your own feelings and clearly state the issues, rather than simply making accusations.

SHARING FEELINGS AND EXPECTATIONS: The only way to avoid accumulating resentment is to openly share feelings. No feeling is too trivial to talk about. Both positive and negative feelings should be shared. It is also important to share your expectations. This way both sides can avoid bitter feelings caused by assumptions and unrealistic expectations.

ACTIVE LISTENING: Listen to each other's message as well as feelings before passing judgment. Avoid jumping to conclusions before understanding the whole situation. It is natural that people usually only view things from their own perspective. If they allow themselves to listen to their spouse without imposing judgment right away, and put themselves in the partner's shoes, more empathy will result.

FOCUS ON THE ISSUE AND NOT THE PERSON: Sometimes husband and wife start to communicate their differences, hoping to come to mutual ground. Yet they end up arguing and lashing out at each other. It is important to stick to the issues that triggered the conflict. Avoid criticism or personal attacks. For example, "I feel taken for granted when you assume that I'll entertain your mother," focuses on a specific issue, instead of "You are so insensitive to my needs and all you think of is your relatives. Your whole family is like that..." The latter statement actually avoids the issue and promotes further conflict.

IF YOU HAVE TO FIGHT, FIGHT FAIRLY

"I hate to argue. She always gets so emotional, so I choose to be silent," Joe said.

No one likes to fight. In fact, most people will do everything to avoid fighting with their partner. Most of us don't realize that fights are necessary, even healthy, sometimes, especially when there are conflicts, disagreements or unresolved issues that get pushed aside without being properly dealt with.

An argument or fight is a channel to bring such things into the open. After all, what people are afraid to talk out, they act out. For example, through broken eye-contact, reduced physical contact, etc. Either way, the unresolved business cannot be ignored.

People attempt to avoid unpleasant confrontations in various ways, all of which can be destructive and eventually cause resentment and destroy intimacy.

SILENCE: This is a powerful and destructive weapon. In a disagreement, if one side lapses into silence it renders the partner helpless. Though this cuts short the argument, the issues are left unresolved.

YIELDING: Sometimes people pay a high price to keep the peace. They appease their partner or agree with him or her, even though deep inside they feel differently. By doing so they not only cheat themselves but also deprive their partner of understanding them. In the short term, life may be smoother because of no disagreement, but in the long run individuals will feel submissive and indignant.

QUICK FIX: Whenever one side brings up a problem or issue which may require discussion, the other blurts out a hasty solution or suggestion. This only shuts off one's partner and indicates, "I am not interested in what you have to say." It also takes away the chance to explore differences which can help prevent future disagreements.

People often believe they have to "win" an argument in order to stop it from dragging on. However, a properly conducted argument can open a channel to constructively confront the issues and differences and to reach mutual consensus. There are rules that should be remembered to turn an argument into a constructive experience.

FOCUS ON THE ISSUE AND NOT THE PERSON: Sometimes couples express their differences or opinions, but before they know it, they end up arguing and lashing out at each other. It is important to stick to the issues and avoid criticism or personal attacks. Identify one's own feelings and give opportunities for the partner to clarify. Then negotiate a mutually acceptable agreement.

A typical fight would sound like:

Mary: "You and your stupid family! I'm sick and tired of seeing them!"

Mike: "If you don't like it, then stay home!"

The constructive argument alternative should be:

Mary: "I'm not happy spending every weekend with your relatives. I feel we have no time for ourselves."

Mike: "I feel it's my obligation, but I didn't know it bothered you so much."

SET A TIME TO FIGHT: Don't catch your partner by surprise. When one or both partners feel discussion is called for, notify the spouse and set an agreeable time so both sides feel prepared psychologically.

DON'T ACCUMULATE UNFINISHED BUSINESS: Once things get put off they can become distorted. Commitment to resolving conflict can also dissipate.

FOCUS ON "HERE AND NOW": During the process of sorting out a disagreement, couples need to remind themselves to deal with the present issue instead of digging out past history as a weapon to attack each other.

BE SPECIFIC: Don't generalize. During arguments individuals tend to be more sensitive or defensive, so it is important to avoid using words like "never", "always", or "should". For example: you "never" support me or you "always" put me down. One needs to be more specific when and how such impressions were received and deal with it directly without letting the anger spill over everything.

Fights or arguments are unavoidable within a relationship. The important thing is a couple's willingness to work through it together and use it as a growth experience. One common complaint is that one or both partners don't have the chance to talk things through before it builds up to the stage of explosion. It will be helpful for a couple to schedule one evening per week for themselves. On that specific night they will not accept any outside invitations and reserve time for each other to talk and be together. They can also use the time to discuss any unresolved business. Commitment to keeping such an evening also shows commitment to marriage as a life-time partnership.

Open and honest communication is the key to a happy marriage. Communication is a two-way street which requires both partners to participate. If mutual communication does not exist, it may be up to one spouse to initiate it. One may feel vulnerable communicating this way and he or she may risk rejection. Yet the risk will be rewarded and serve as a catalyst for the partner to open up as well. It is better to take a risk than to give up the chance for a better marriage.

Afterword

Seeking help

SEEKING HELP ABROAD

THE PURPOSE OF this book is to help you to identify some of the problems you may encounter while living abroad. By understanding and following the recommendations in the preceding chapters, you can learn to help yourself to cope with these issues. However, for some people professional help will be both beneficial and advisable.

Looking for psychological help in a foreign country can be an aggravating and confusing search. How do you find out who is providing such services? Are these people qualified or even trained? How can you tell the difference?

When living in a foreign country where you speak the language, you will likely find many choices of mental health professionals. The question, however, is how to locate and choose someone who can understand your problems as a foreigner, and whose training, methods and cultural understanding are all suitable for helping you.

If you live in a country where you are not fluent in the language, or if you prefer treatment in your native language, clearly your choices are much more limited. Among larger expatriate communities you are likely to find a few people offering psychological services in English, and, to a lesser extent, in other languages.

Before going further, it helps to understand exactly what the different types of mental health practitioners are and what they can and cannot do.

"I'm having problems with my wife. I think I need a psychiatrist," a middle-aged man said. He imagines himself in a Woody Allen movie, lying on the couch and talking about his past. Meanwhile, a balding man with a pointed beard and spectacles, says "Ja, ja," with a German accent, while sitting beside him jotting notes.

In fact, a psychiatrist is not necessarily the answer for personal problems, especially those involving emotional, family, personal growth or relationship issues.

There are various mental health professionals who provide different forms of treatment. These include Psychiatrists, Psychologists, Family Therapists and Clinical Social Workers. Unfortunately, there are some misconceptions about who does what.

Let's take an overview of different types of mental health practitioners. It is not easy to totally distinguish their roles from one another because many have overlapping functions and expertise. They can be broadly placed into two groups: psychiatrists and psychotherapists.

PSYCHIATRISTS are medical doctors whose specialty is treatment of mental illness. Examples of mental illnesses include schizophrenia, personality disorders, psychosis and chemical imbalance in the brain. Psychiatric treatment very often includes short or long-term medication. Though the traditional picture of a psychiatrist from Freud's time was a person who provided psychoanalysis, this is not commonly practiced in a modern psychiatric setting. Some psychiatrists do offer counseling, though in actual practice this is rarely their specialty.

PSYCHOTHERAPIST is a broad term for therapists who provide treatment for mental and emotional problems — as opposed to mental illnesses—by applying various psycho- therapeutic techniques. This category includes Psychologists, Family Therapists and Clinical Social Workers.

PSYCHOLOGISTS work in various specialties, includ- ing Clinical, Educational and Industrial Psychologists. Generally, Educational and Industrial Psychologists do research, testing and education. Clinical Psychologists or Counseling Psychologists provide psychological counsel- ing to treat psychological, mental and emotional disorders for individual patients. Most psychologists have PhD-level training.

MARRIAGE & FAMILY THERAPISTS similarly treat psychological and emotional problems. They generally look at a patient's family background and dynamics to gain insight into individual problems and behavior. This field developed in the USA in the 1960s, and is widely recognized and practiced in North America, Australia and Europe. In those places, specialized Master's Degree training is required for licensing.

CLINICAL SOCIAL WORKERS generally deal with crisis intervention and short-term therapy, though increas- ingly they also provide long-term therapy to individuals, families or groups. Clinical Social Workers, as opposed to other social workers, also tend to require Master's Degrees in order to practice.

How do you choose among all these practitioners when you have a problem? There is no unequivocal answer. The above three types of psychotherapists (excluding psychiatrists) have similar roles, their main differences being in educational background and training. In a private practice setting, all provide nearly identical services. You should feel confident in consulting a Psychologist, Family Therapist or Clinical Social Worker for most problems. A genuine professional will tell you up-front whether they can help you with your issue.

It is important to distinguish between mental illness and other emotional problems. If you suspect that mental illness is the issue, a psychiatrist is the first source to consult. For family and personal emotional problems, any of the three categories of psychotherapist will be able to assess the problem and help you to proceed.

Psychotherapists are not medical doctors and may not prescribe medication. When a qualified psychotherapist feels an individual may require medication, he or she will refer the person to a psychiatrist for evaluation. Likewise. if a psychiatrist thinks counseling is recommended, he or she will usually refer the patient to a trusted psychotherapist.

How do I know if they're qualified?

Unfortunately, in many countries the field of psychological services is unregulated. Many places lack even a professional governing body to monitor those who provide psychological treatment. The quality of psychological services can be quite varied, ranging from the genuinely qualified to the inadequately trained, and even to outright charlatans out to steal your money.

This is especially so among expatriate communities, where resources are limited. There are often many enterprising but untrained individuals offering counseling after having taken a brief course, or coming from other human service professions such as nursing, believing that their rapport with people is qualification enough. Unfortunately, expat communities are a breeding ground for amateur and unprofessional practice which can lead to serious harm.

Psychological training requires far more than just "being good with people" or attending a training seminar. To practice legally in most developed countries, Psychologists, Family Therapists, and Clinical Social Workers all require accredited university training plus at least two years of internship. Usually a license or other professional registration is required to practice.

To protect your mental welfare, and eliminate some of the pitfalls in the search for a qualified and professional mental health therapist, you can start by consulting a few resources.

REFERRAL RESOURCES

A number of sources maintain referral lists of qualified mental health practitioners. Following are some good places to try:

YOUR COUNTRY'S CONSULAR OFFICE: See whether their in-house medical officer can give you names of recommended therapists. In most cases when a country does employ a psychiatrist or psychologist to serve their diplomatic staff, he or she serves an entire region, and is not full-time in any one consulate. Such a person normally does not provide service to civilians. Therefore, if you are a diplomatic family member seeking regular weekly therapy, or if you are a non-diplomat, you will have to seek help in the local community. Some consulates do maintain a referral list of mental health professionals, though many do not.

INTERNATIONAL SCHOOLS: Contact the head guidance counselor. International schools often keep on retainer a qualified psychologist who provides short-term therapy for students who have been referred to him or her. Guidance counselors usually maintain lists of other mental health practitioners, if any, in the community. Normally only well-experienced, highly-qualified practitioners would be on a school counselor's referral list.

PSYCHOLOGICAL SOCIETY: If there is a national or local Psychological Society or Association, they may have a referral list or at least a list of members. Often membership in such societies is heavily weighted toward academics and researchers, so it may take some weeding through such a list to find an actual practitioner. Obviously, anyone on the list would have met legitimate professional requirements.

DOCTORS: Ask your physician for names he or she can suggest or if he knows of a local mental health guide which may list the qualified practicing therapists.

CLERGY: Religious leaders can be helpful resources. Many clerics receive training in counseling and offer this service to their parishioners. In some communities, a pastor, priest or rabbi may be the only resource available. Clerics would most likely be aware of lay practitioners in the area, and not necessarily only ones of their own religious persuasion.

HELP LINES: The Samaritans or established self-help groups like Alcoholics Anonymous, if there is a chapter that operates in your language, often have a psychological consultant affiliated with the group.

COMMUNITY ADVICE BUREAUS: Many expatriate communities have one. See whether they have a list of recommended mental health practitioners.

Often the best resource is a trusted friend or colleague who has been through therapy and been satisfied with the treatment. Be careful, though. Make sure you are referred by someone who has been through therapy or has professional knowledge of the therapist, and who is not just drumming up business for an acquaintance who may or may not be qualified.

CHECK THEIR CREDENTIALS!

Whether you've been referred to somebody or you've found her or him yourself, it still pays to be certain.

The most important criterion is to seek someone you feel comfortable working with. Don't be shy about asking questions about her or his training and credentials. Don't be persuaded by a wall full of certificates. Read them closely or ask questions directly. Sometimes people receive diploma-like certificates after a weekend training seminar.

- How long has she or he been practicing in the field?

- How long has he or she been practicing in this country?

- What experience do they have in working with expatriates?

- Is she or he certified or licensed in the country they originally come from or were trained in?

- Does he or she feel competent with the type of problem you are experiencing?

Finally, beware of advertisements promising quick cures for psychological or personal problems. No genuine therapist will ever make such a claim. After all, problems that build up over many years also require time to heal.

When you are ready to deal with your personal problems, take it seriously and seek a legitimate person to help you. Remember: the first step in therapy is learning to take the responsibility to help yourself.

About the author

Dr. Cathy Tsang-Feign is a leading expert in the field of expatriate and cross-cultural psychology, based on decades of experience working with international executives and diplomats and their families in North America, Europe, Asia and Australia.

She holds Master's Degrees in Counseling and Family Therapy and a PhD in Psychology. She has practised professionally in Los Angeles and Atlanta, as well as London's Harley Street, and currently runs a private practice in Hong Kong. She travels extensively to provide training and assessments for international corporations and government organizations.

She is a former columnist on family psychology for the *South China Morning Post* and *American in Britain.*

She is married with two children and is an avid gardener and beekeeper in her spare time.

For more information, visit her website:

WWW.CATHYFEIGN.COM

Printed in Great Britain
by Amazon.co.uk, Ltd.,
Marston Gate.